The Noble
And
Great Ones

**IT'S NOT ABOUT PROPORTIONS,
IT'S WHAT'S IN THE GLASS
THAT MATTERS MOST**

Mark Colo

Caliente Press

The Noble and Great Ones

It's Not About Proportions,
It's What's In The Glass That Matters Most

ISBN 978-1-943702-94-7 (Paperback)
979-1-943702-95-4 (Kindle)

Caliente Press
1775 E. Palm Canyon Drive, Suite 110-198
Palm Springs, CA 92264
www.CalientePress.com

Ordering Information: Special discounts are available on quantity purchases by corporations, associations, and others. For details, contact the "Special Sales Department" at the address above.

Book Layout ©2017 BookDesignTemplates.com

Cover Design: Héctor Castañeda

Scripture quotations from The Authorized (King James) Version.
Rights in the Authorized Version in the United Kingdom are vested in the Crown.
Reproduced by permission of the Crown's patentee, Cambridge University Press.

Mark has been an inspirational being and friend in my life for many years. It wasn't until I read his book, *The Noble and Great Ones*, that I realized why he was such an important part of my life. His book offers keen and deep insight into life and how we should deal with the events and experiences we have had or will have going forward.

His Five Credos provide insight, knowledge and better understanding to our life experiences.

1) "The only constant is change. Embrace it."

2) "If you think things cannot get worse, you're wrong! Endure it."

3) "Control is an illusion. Let go of it."

4) "Life isn't always fair. Accept it."

5) "There are no coincidences in life, just miracles."

When life's events are framed by these five credos, we each can have a better understanding of life and our mission here on this earth.

Thank you Mark for being my friend and for sharing such wonderful incites and thoughts on life to help me and so many others. It will have a positive influence in the lives of those who read this important work.

John McCoy
Friend/Retired Disneyland International Executive

Although I grew up in Phoenix and had a lot of friends of the LDS Faith, I never knew much about it. I learned a lot from this book and it is amazing to see how you have looked upward and found peace in faith.

I never knew there was no "cure" for Parkinson's Disease, but it is great to see the progress that scientists have made. I am very interested in continuing to learn about it and support the research that is happening.

I loved all of the life lessons you shared and the one that resonated with me the most was identifying the different "layers" in my life that have hardened and shaped who I am today.

Thank you again for sharing with me this book and I can't wait to read your next one.

Heidi Liou
Strategic Partnerships Manager at Supermoves

I have known Mark for many years. We work together with his foundation. As you better understand how Mark has overcome his adversities of life, you will come to better understand why I believe he is one of the Noble and Great Ones. He would never say it because he is too humble. But as Mark indicates in his Preface, what makes Noble and Great Ones is their Credos. That is what makes Mark so different – his Credos. As you read his book, *The Noble and Great Ones*, I hope that the stories Mark relates will inspire you to reach higher and to be better – that you will see within yourself a Noble and Great one!

Scott G. Scoville
Retired Deputy District Attorney
County of Orange

In the Preface, Mark Colo tells us about his daily ritual and how it prepares him for his day. Up early, he uses the time for thinking, for exercise, connection to his God, for learning something each day, feeling alive. Stop! Right now it appears I'll be telling you about how strong and powerful this guy is.

Nope...it's all about Mark and how he has dealt with a sudden neuro adversity and many challenges. Read the Preface and you will find guidance and very likely you will also find peace. But there's more to the story. Enjoy the book and also, see this video https://findneurohelp.org

Ed Cohen
Broadcast Host
Global-TV Talkshow™

Contents

Dedication

My wife Mary
and our three children
Rachel, Josh, and Lauren
who have supported me in all my crazy ideas,
lifted me up when I was down,
and helped me to find my true identity and purpose in life.

Failure will never overtake me,
if my determination to succeed
is strong enough.

Og Mandino

Preface

It is 5:00 on a Monday morning. I have just exited my home's front door here in Irvine, CA, stepped down a shallow porch step, and walked 12 paces to a low retaining wall in my front courtyard. Here I sit each morning to have my daily prayer, a ritual I have grown to treasure. It is a way for me to reconnect with my Heavenly Father, express my gratitude, ask how I am doing, seek His wisdom, and ask for His guidance in my life.

This moment of peace, perspective, and gratitude occurs before the sun rises, traffic noises crowd the air, and email or text messages demand attention. Morning prayer has become an invaluable and indispensable practice that has helped me to remember who I am, where I am heading, and, most importantly, who it is that can get me there.

When my prayer is complete, I walk 30 paces to a side gate in our cul-de-sac that opens onto a rectangular walking path running the perimeter of my neighborhood, a distance of about 1.3 miles round trip. The walk takes me about 30 minutes, provided the squirrels along the walkway are not putting on a show. Walking the trail has become my second favorite morning ritual. The journey begins by inserting my noise-canceling Air Pods and selecting the morning listening genre from a playlist that comprises audio scripture, a bestselling book, pre-recorded Ted Talks, or an interesting podcast. Once chosen, I hit play and am on my way.

This secondary ritual of morning worship I refer to as my "PR Moment." It has nothing to do with image, brand reputation, or social relations. This PR acronym stands for "Personal Revelation." It comes through the Holy Ghost, and it is available to every man, woman, and child of God, regardless of race, religion, color, creed, wealth, or social status. We are all God's children, and by virtue of divine origin, there is nobility and greatness within each of us.

PR, as the acronym implies, is personal. Revelation can come to each of us in a myriad of ways. It can come through whisperings of the spirit, impressions, by enlightenment as we read the scriptures, in dreams, and through the testimony of others.

The impact of waking up an hour earlier to begin the day with prayer, peace, and fresh perspective can dramatically impact our mental, physical, and spiritual outlook on life. The residual benefits of making PR a daily habit include: Peace, Purpose, Power, Progress, Protection, Patience, Persistence, Perspective, Penitence, and Personal Identity.

These Ten Pillars of PR are qualities that protect us, help us understand personal trials, manage adversity, and build a more meaningful and purposeful life. No matter what challenges we face in mortality, it is essential that we always remember, "It's not about proportions, it's what's in the glass that matters most."

A Difficult Beginning

Three questions have puzzled me since my adolescent years. First, "Why are we born into our particular family?" Second, "Why are the personalities in our families so different?" And third, "Why do some people's lives seem so easy, while others' lives appear nearly impossible to bear?"

By the time you finish reading *The Noble and Great Ones*, you will know the answers to these puzzling questions. The source through which we can find answers to our deepest and most perplexing queries is our Father in Heaven. Access to revelation is granted to all those who humble themselves before God, who desire to know Him, and are willing to make the necessary changes to please Him. The gateway is through heartfelt prayer and the medium is the impressions you receive from the Spirit of God. PR is available to all those who desire to change or understand their present circumstance.

Call Me Rumpelstiltskin

Prayer and PR came to me early in life, and in no small measure due to the family distress and discord my brother Paul and I each experienced from birth.

Our parents divorced when I was three years of age. My father would later enlighten me on the reason. He was physically and emotionally disconnected, telling me just four years before his passing that he never wanted children. "It was your mother's idea," he said. Then it dawned on me why he told Paul and me to stop calling him Dad. "Call me Rumpelstiltskin," he would say. He longed for a whimsical, come and go as you would like, no strings attached lifestyle. So for my brother and me, he became a make-believe creature that would pop in from time to time.

In the ten years following our parent's divorce, our small family of three would move seven times. When I turned 14, my mother met and married her second husband, an LAPD motorcycle police officer named Gary. This second marriage was not much better than the first. Our come and go when you wish lifestyle in short order was replaced by a Marine barrack for delinquent kids. This new rooster in the henhouse introduced curfews, corporal punishment, and threats that would scare Paul and me into non-endearing submission. I recall feeling as though we were second-class citizens with a generous portion of self-pity. In essence, we braced for what was doomed to be a second abandonment at some point in the future.

To this point, my life had been fairly simple and somewhat non-eventful. That was until an event repeatedly occurred during my adolescent years, which shattered my confidence, destroyed my self-worth, and elevated my insecurities to a level 10 earthquake on the emotional Richter Scale.

The trial that I am referring to was a series of pre-teen sexual molestations perpetrated and executed by an older gay half-brother who had been assigned to keep an eye on us while our father, aka Rumpelstiltskin, was teaching at a local university in Los Angeles, CA. The advances and encounters from this custodial predator occurred for several years until one day my dad returned home to the apartment unexpectantly and caught him doing an incriminating striptease in the hall doorway. He reacted with a life-threatening, "I will beat you to a pulp if I ever catch you doing this again."

Life events such as these can be crippling on the psyche and taxing on the soul. In my case, the residual fallout was a life living under the degrading and morass-like fog that is a residual mixture of fear, apathy, and doubt (or FAD as I often refer to this condition). Unfortunately, FAD is becoming increasingly rampant among our youth as they navigate this experience we call life. Unlike most fads, it does not pass quickly.

The Turning Point

In January 1977, at 19 years of age, I left my home in sunny Southern California to serve a two-year service mission in

Scotland and Northern Ireland during that region's intense civil unrest.

Looking back on that time, I find it miraculous that I would be called to serve in the birthplace of James Irvine II, the original owner of one of the largest real estate empires in the world, a landmass five times the size of Manhattan and the man whom the city of Irvine is named. James Irvine II migrated to Myford, CA, from County Down, the very place where I served the first 11 months of my mission. What are the odds of that? Amazingly, the city of Irvine is where I would work, live, and raise my family for nearly 30 years of my life!

By virtue of the unique experiences I had in these two countries while serving the Scots and Irish, I began to form what would become my five credos of life:

1. *"The only constant is change. Embrace it."* The Irish had a saying they would share with visitors to their country as an icebreaker, "If you don't like the weather, wait five minutes." Those who have been to the Emerald Isle can attest that the weather there is unpredictable.

    The same can be said about life. Whatever twists and turns you have along the way, embrace them and learn from them.

2. *"If you think things cannot get worse, you're wrong! Endure it."* That is not to say you are a pessimist. Life is often unpredictable. Any of us could find ourselves living in a cardboard box on the side of a road if a series of unfortunate events occur in sequence (i.e., you lose your job, you have no family support, you learn you have a chronic or terminal illness, the bills are piling up, etc.). If you think these things could never

happen, study and ponder the life of Job. There is an entire book written about this faithful disciple of Christ.

3. *"Control is an illusion. Let go of it."* One of the most common Parkinson's symptoms is "a resting tremor." It is most easily recognized by an involuntary shaking of an appendage. It typically begins in a single finger, then spreads throughout the hand, and then the arm. What is most unusual is that when you try to control the condition, or you are under added stress, the tremor is magnified. Let go of control!

4. *"Life isn't always fair. Accept it."* The rain falls on the Just and the Unjust. There is not always an easy answer to why some good people have trials and some bad people appear to have everything. Save your energy on this one and just accept it.

5. *"There are no coincidences in life, just miracles."* See the miracle.

The Day the Earth Shook

Shortly following my 48th birthday, I noticed an unusual physical change occurring in my right pinky finger as it began to quiver on its own. It was especially apparent when I was under stress, typically while conducting a meeting or giving a talk at church. Speaking in front of groups with a few hundred members might seem like enough to make anyone's hands shake, but only my right hand was affected.

I convinced myself this new phenomenon must be due to a pinched nerve or spinal irregularity. This unique event prompted me to make an appointment post-haste to see my general MD. He recommended that I meet with a neurologist.

The neurologist performed a series of tests that included electro-analysis and observing me walking down a hallway. His diagnosis on that day was he felt my symptoms were pre-Parkinsonian.

I recall leaving the examination room in a daze of disbelief. "Was that a dream?" I asked myself. "Did that really just happen?"

Exiting the hospital, I felt as though the weight of the world had just been placed upon my shoulders. Profound sadness and some bitterness began to crowd my thoughts. Why me? What have I done to deserve this? My mind began spinning to the past in search of answers and into the future imagining what this life would now become. Loneliness, fear, and doubt began to creep into my thoughts. Without exception, this was the greatest blow to my peace of mind and sense of self-worth that I had ever experienced.

At that time, I was 48 years old, the sole provider for our family that included three children under ten years of age. No pressure here, right?

I was completely unprepared for the news I received that day. There was no one there to catch my fall. No one there to be my advocate. No one there to console me. There simply was no one there at all.

This, and many other similar experiences, compelled me to create FIND NEURO HELP, a 501(c) (3) charity committed to funding neurological research groups that reflect the greatest promise in finding cures for the various chronic illnesses we support. FIND NEURO HELP also provides help to those who have these diseases find relief and hope.

My first book, *Peace With Parkinson's: It is Called a Resting Tremor, Not an Earthquake,* was written to provide help, hope, and advocacy for individuals impacted by Parkinson's and other life-altering neuro-diseases. This second book you are reading was written to help those who struggle to recognize the uniqueness within, reach their true potential, and have joy. No do-overs, no regrets. Just agency and accountability.

Today, my wife Mary and I live in Irvine, California, a city known for its academia and low crime. There is a world-class university nearby called UC Irvine, and many of the streets here bear names of universities around the U.S, such as Harvard, Yale, Stanford, and several others. There is even a high school that supports this emphasis on higher academics named University High School.

We first moved to Irvine 12 years ago, after living the prior 18 years in the beachside community of Newport Coast. Nestled in the hills overlooking Newport Beach Harbor, Newport Coast was often referred to as the Irvine Company's gem property and as the "Beverly Hills of Orange County." Geographically the two cities are adjacent to one another. The Irvine Company owns both parcels of land.

We opted to relocate to Irvine for several primary reasons. First was for the benefit of our children, consisting of Rachel, Joshua, Lauren, and our dog Quincy, the largest Cockapoo on the planet. We found a much larger youth contingency in Irvine and we believed it would be a much better social fit for them.

Second, we wanted to give our children a competitive educational head start for their future. Third, we felt that moving to a lower rent community would shield them from a sense of entitlement and the stigma of "keeping up with the Jones." Fourth, it made sense at the time to relocate to a lower cost of living community to reduce the financial pressures on me due to my diagnosis of early-onset Parkinson's Disease.

Between Mary and me, we had not given much thought to the impact the move would have on our children. We learned the hard way.

Credos are Mantras on Steroids

A mantra is a saying or slogan used frequently to help us make sense of the mistakes we make in life.

There are several mantras I have heard ringing in my ears throughout my life. The first is, "There are those that make things happen, those that watch things happen, and those that wonder what happened." The odds are fairly high that we all drift into and out of these three phases on a regular basis. I believe that when an outcome is within our control, we instinctively focus on the first group. The second category is for moviegoers and the third category is the place that the painful and difficult lessons of life occur. It is a place that the Average Joe calls his or her home.

The second mantra is, "Hindsight is 20/20." The right choices and outcomes of our actions might have had a better aftermath had our vision been clearer. The key word is "might." The reality of life is that the collateral damage we incur is often beyond our control.

The third, and final, mantra is, "This too shall pass." These were my grandmother's words of encouragement she would impart to me whenever we were together. She must have seen something that I did not see.

Mantras may have their place in helping us feel better about a mistake, but they are a bandage solution at best. A credo, on the other hand, is a mantra on steroids. It is a principle that brings clarity, focus, and action. A credo is like a verb versus a noun, a vaccine versus a virus, and freedom versus imprisonment. Credos are an enabling and effective way to change perspective and cope with life's setbacks and vicissitudes.

As fate would have it, the five credos shared previously, along with my faith in Jesus Christ, have been a source of encouragement and strength for me in managing the challenges of Parkinson's Disease.

As you read the Noble and Great ones, you will be introduced to rulers of their craft, individuals who could elevate their game to the highest level of performance. These purposefully driven, remarkably persistent, and resilient champions had the resolve to press forward when most others would have quit. What made the difference? Credos!

Introduction

For most readers, the title of *The Noble and Great Ones*, or NGO in its abbreviated form, will be unfamiliar. Suppose you were to guess the origin of this distinguished title. In that case, your thoughts might drift back to medieval times when knights were coroneted for acts of bravery and men like William Wallace were revered for their courage and fearlessness in fighting for freedom from tyranny.

If you are analytical, as I am, you may ponder each of these descriptive words independently and reflect on their associated meaning. Noble and Great are adjectives used in this manuscript to describe a plural noun, meaning there are one or more persons, places, or things associated with or identified by these two descriptive words.

Webster's Dictionary defines Noble as "having, showing, or coming from personal qualities that people admire (such as honesty, generosity, courage, humility, etc.). The full definition found in Webster's Online Dictionary includes additional phrases such as "possessing outstanding qualities," "of high birth," or "exalted rank." Noble also refers to anyone who possesses nobility and displays superiority of mind, character, morals, or ideals. Noble is most often used to describe qualities of royalty as an act or condition of moral distinction, as in he or she is a "Noble Man or Noble Woman," or something is a "Noble Act or a Noble Deed."

Great is defined by Webster's as "notably large, large in number or measure, remarkable in magnitude, degree or effectiveness." Other definitions include "full of emotion," "chief or preeminent over others," and "remarkably skilled." Great is most frequently used to describe personal accomplishments such as "he is a great person," or "he helped build a great city," or the artist produced a "great painting." It can also be used as a personal endorsement for previous accomplishments as in, "his greatness precedes him."

Finally, the word "Ones" is used to reference members of this distinctive group of people.

For simplicity and brevity purposes, I will refer to these uniquely gifted and passionately driven individuals as NGOs.

Nobility vs. Greatness – Sequence Matters

The sequential order of these two adjectives, and their respective influence on one another, is significant and a constituent principle upon which this book was written. Nobility was at the heart of the creation and the redemption and salvation of mankind. It is also at the core of our identity and purpose here in mortality.

Nobility is not just about virtue. It is a governing force in the universe with the power, capacity, and influence to change mediocrity into excellence, apathy into meaningful purpose, despair into hope, and hatred into a love of all mankind.

Nobility is self-deprecating, It impels its bearer to sacrifice personal gains and immediate gratification for the long-term goodwill of others. There is no prejudice, bias, self-righteous judgment, pride, anger, or personal agendas found in nobility.

History records that the pursuit of greatness, without the guiding influence of nobility, is, in most instances, self-serving, self-absorbing, and self-condemning. Nobility, on the other hand, is greatness in and of itself. If you should ever find yourself facing an important decision that promises greatness at the expense of nobility, choose the latter and you will have already attained the first.

Nobility is at the heart of some of the greatest acts known to mankind. *The Noble and Great Ones* was written to recognize individuals who became men and women of stature, nobility, and greatness by virtue of their lives and the standards they maintained. The commitment, contributions, and legacies they left for their posterity and humanity saved lives, brought hope to millions, and were a lasting type of nobility and greatness.

The Devil's Brigade

In *The Noble and Great Ones*, you will find individuals who possessed great talent and the ability to impact humanity significantly. Unfortunately, with a focus only on the allure of greatness, they tragically chose the opposite direction. By abusing their power and misusing their agency, these fallen ones gradually extinguished the last photon of illumination within them. In doing so, they committed some of the most heinous and darkest acts in history.

Their cruelty, treachery, and barbarian passions for power and self-indulgence led them to abandon any moral virtue they may have possessed. You may ponder why these individuals turned from the light they once had to forfeit the measure of their creation. The plaguing memory of their lives will forever be a stain on humanity that will echo through the eternities.

NGO Characteristics

Based upon the aforementioned definitions and the individual and collective meanings of the five words that comprise this distinctive classification, we can conclude that inclusion into this outstanding and prominent collection of overachievers would require a noble heart, pure intent, a passionate desire to rise above mediocracy and make a significant impact for good in the lives of others, their communities, and humanity.

NGOs generally show signs of their nobility and greatness early in life. This provides them with a head start in filling the measure of their creation and feeling the exuberance and joy that comes from personal triumph and reaching their true potential.

Due to the nobility and greatness within NGOs and their insatiable desires to test their limits, they are often described by others as uniquely gifted, passionately driven, relentlessly persistent, and over-achieving rebels with a cause. Once the fire has been lit within them, and their goals are in sight, pity the person who stands in their way.

NGOs, by their very nature, embrace virtuous qualities that most people admire. Their actions spring from the belief that all men are created equally, and the worth of souls is great. NGOs are driven and sustained by a purposeful sense of identity, a love for their fellow man, and a duty to God.

NGOs have the authentic, limitless, and never-ending ability to bond quickly, effortlessly, and trustworthily. This is a byproduct of their own first-hand experiences in bearing trials themselves. It is also the byproduct and residual blessing of having empathy toward others that adversity can forge within our own lives. Their words of comfort, compassion, purpose, and potential have iron.

The quality of judgment they possess and their ability to instantaneously connect, console, and relate to the physically afflicted, the socially outcast, and the homeless is forged in the furnace of their own physical, mental, and emotional trials. It also results from the humbling handicaps, shortcomings, and lessons they have learned.

NGOs emulate empathy, inspire hope, and know precisely how, what, when, where, why, and whom to succor. The exact moment and time of their words of encouragement, motivation, and inspiration will greatly impact the individuals who need their wisdom and encouragement the most.

NGOs are goal-driven game-changers. They have unyielding courage, commitment, and the ability to stay the course in attaining their goals. They can eat adversity for breakfast, lunch, and dinner and leave room for dessert. They use adversity as an opportunity to gain added wisdom, strength, and courage for the glory of God. NGOs are overachievers who go far beyond the "just here today to collect a paycheck" and "that's not in my job description" group mentality. NGOs live purposefully driven lives and inspire others to do the same.

NGO Humility

Although it is not uncommon to find NGOs on the cover of *Sports Illustrated*, *National Geographic*, or *Forbes*, fame, fortune, and visibility are rarely the driving forces behind their performances and achievements. In fact, it is not uncommon to find NGOs downplaying their accomplishments, avoiding the limelight from personal success, and dodging recognition or adoration.

In large part, this results from their humility, modesty, and the moral compasses by which they are led. No matter how great their accomplishments may be, NGOs never lose sight of the benefactor for their success. The bearer of nobility instinctively uses their talents to bless and serve the lives of others. The nobility within themselves protects them from succumbing to self-aggrandizing greatness. When one places nobility first, the proper path to greatness can be revealed. For nobility, in and of itself, is greatness. We will expand upon the innate qualities of these humble giants in the chapter *The Unsung Heroes*.

The Noble and Great Ones was written to accentuate individuals of high moral distinction whose deeds, actions, and achievements deserve recognition and the respect of others. In some instances, they lived reclusive lives, avoiding the media and paparazzi. In other instances, they were "rebels with a cause." Whether the catalyst behind their passions to persist was fame, fortune, freedom, or self-driven, you will read about individuals with remarkable talents and abilities whose lives and contributions have made a lasting impression and impact on themselves, our lives, and the future of humanity.

As you read *The Noble and Great Ones*, you will be introduced to individuals who possessed tremendous talent, ability, and fortitude. These remarkable overachievers all share four common traits. First, they recognize their giftedness and use it to their advantage early in life. Second, they are relentless in honing their unique skills. Third, they live lives of servitude fit for nobility, always taking the high road and placing the needs of others before their own. Fourth, they live gratefully and graciously, giving God and their mentors credit and giving back to their communities.

The Power of Acronyms

What is an Acronym? An acronym is an abbreviation describing a series of words. One example is the word ACRONYM itself that could represent: A Coded Reference of Names Yielding Meaning.

Acronyms can help us remember important principles and meaningful habits for self-improvement. They can warn us of detrimental and destructive habits and behaviors. And they can condense our vocabulary when we are in a hurry, such as OK, LOL, CMB, LVM, and OMG. Or, on the darker side, KMN and IHM.

By the time you finish reading *The Noble and Great Ones*, you will have learned nearly a dozen easy-to-memorize acronyms you can use as daily reminders to help shield you from negativity and improve your positivity and spirituality. Many of these acronyms are keys to self-discovery and self-improvement. Others can help guide and direct you in discovering your true identity, thereby revealing and releasing gifts and talents within you.

Committing these acronyms to memory and applying them can bring you hope, purpose, happiness, and joy. These meaningful phrases can shield you from harm and act as a warning that you are on dangerous ground that may result in pain, suffering, and even despair. These particular acronyms can protect you from errant thoughts and actions that have the power to rob you of your true identity and purpose.

Here are ten of the acronyms that will be presented in this book. Six of them will foster the discovery of your true identity; four of them can crush it.

B.U.M.P.E.R.

D.E.S.P.A.I.R.

E.A.S.I.E.R.

F.A.D.

G.O.D.H.O.O.D.

H.O.P.E.

O.P.T.I.M.I.S.M.

P.E.S.S.I.M.I.S.M.

P.E.S.T.U.O.U.S.

S.O.A.P.

CHAPTER 1

Origins and Characteristics of Noble and Great Ones

T he title of NGO came by way of a discovery in 1831 when explorer and archeologist Antonio Lebolo was excavating a tomb in the ancient city of Thebes, near modern-day Luxor, Egypt. Inside the tomb were several hundred mummies, most of which were in an unsalvageable condition. Lebolo successfully excavated eleven of these mummies and numerous parchment scrolls. Unfortunately, while en route to Paris, he became ill and died in Trieste, Italy.

Evidence suggests that before Lebolo died, he bequeathed the artifacts to his nephew Michael Chandler. The shipment was mistakenly shipped to Chandler in Dublin, Ireland, where Chandler lived prior to relocating to live in the United States. The shipment was then rerouted to New York and made its way into Chandler's hands sometime in the spring of 1833.

Chandler toured the United States with his new exhibit with the hope of selling them to the highest bidder. When the exhibit arrived in Kirtland, Ohio, Joseph Smith, referred to as the first Prophet of this dispensation and the founder of The Church of Jesus Christ of Latter-day Saints, along with several other members of that faith, chipped in and purchased the scrolls. Smith, who had previously translated a similar language, but by contrast to parchment, was inscribed on gold plates.

The contents of the scrolls are compiled in *The Pearl of Great Price*, a record that brings added insight into the Prophet Abraham's life and reveals several of his recorded visions. *The Pearl of Great Price*, *The Book of Mormon* (the aforementioned record), the *Holy Bible* (KJV), and the *Doctrine and Covenants* comprise the church's early history. In the recorded revelation from the Prophet Joseph Smith, these represent the four primary cannons of scripture in the LDS faith.

From an antiquity perspective, the scrolls bearing our book title are estimated to have been placed in the tomb of their discovery between 300 BC and 100 BC. From an eternal perspective, once translated, the scrolls revealed that Abraham saw the Noble and Great Ones existed in a premortal existence before the earth was formed.

Abraham gave these insights into the characteristics and nature of NGOs by describing them in this way, "I observed that they were also among them The Noble and Great Ones who were chosen in the beginning to be rulers in the Church of God. Before their mortal birth, they, with "many others," received their first lessons in the world of spirits and were prepared to come forth in the time of the Lord to labor in his vineyard for the salvation of the souls of men."

Abraham added further noble characteristics of NGOs by adding, "Now the Lord had shown unto me, Abraham, the intelligences that were organized before the world was; and among all these there were many of the noble and great ones; And God saw these souls that they were good, and he stood in the midst of them, and he said: These I will make my rulers; for he stood among those that were spirits, and he saw that they were good; and he said unto me: Abraham, thou art one of them; thou wast chosen before thou wast born." (Abraham 3:22-23)

Those of this elite class are referred to as the Noble and Great Ones. Unlike monarchs that may inherit their power, status, or rank by ancestry and birthright, NGOs attain their respect the old-fashioned way: they earn it.

NGO Testing

Whether an NGO had a pre-understanding of the specific challenges they would face in mortality, they knew that earth life would not be easy, but necessary for their eternal progression. Because of their desire to please their Heavenly Father and express the inherent nobility and greatness within them, they chose to experience the vicissitudes of life, enter mortality, and experience the endless trials, adversities, and sorrows that mortality can inflict, as well as the happiness, joy, and sense of fulfillment it can also bring into our lives.

There is purpose in the trials we receive here in mortality on earth. The Peter Principle is this, "That the trial of your faith, being much more precious than of gold that perished, though it be tried with fire, might be found unto praise and honor and glory at the appearing of Jesus Christ." (1 Peter 7)

The specific reasons behind the adversity we experience and our true purpose in coming here will be covered in the chapter *A Purpose-Full Life.*

NGO Features and Characteristics

NGOs come in all shapes, sizes, assortments, and venues. They can be large, small, short or tall, rich or poor, male or female. They are found within every culture, ancestry, and religion. They may be born into impoverished circumstances, wealth, anarchy, or oppression. Regardless of their birth circumstances, they have the ability to remain optimistic, faithful, and resilient. They believe in their abilities and have faith that God will guide them and sustain them in fulfilling the measure of their creation and purpose.

NGOs press forward relentlessly and resiliently. The more setbacks they have, the more life lessons they learn, and the more apt they are to succeed. They recognize that the lower they may fall, the higher they can reach. They remain grateful in whatever situations or circumstances befall them. NGOs, like most of us, experience moments of discouragement, sadness, and even depression. But they do not use these moments as permission to wallow in the mire of self-pity. Rather, they remain optimistic and grateful, relentlessly pressing forward until they achieve their goals and purposes.

NGOs have the unique advantage of seeing the world as if through a different lens. The goals, objectives, or records we may deem doubtful or impossible to surpass or achieve, they see as possible and achievable. NGOs have the childlike ability to find happiness and joy in doing what you or I might deem ordinary or superfluous. They exhibit childlike faith in situations and circumstances most of us would deem as dire. They exude courage when all odds are against them and there is no relief in sight. NGOs are patient, long-suffering, and resilient, especially when faced with physical, mental, and emotional suffering.

Although they may spend their adolescent years in relative obscurity, they can appear instantaneously as flag bearers with a purpose. Their patriotism and nobility in defending a noble cause and foregoing their own personal rights for doing what is right can brand them as "rebels with a cause."

NGOs never give up and never surrender. They are on an evolutionary path of forward motion, increasing velocity, and vertical trajectory of continual improvement and self-mastery.

NGOs are the happiest when they are uplifting and serving others. Their deepest joy comes from helping others to recognize their self-worth and true potential.

All For One, And One For All

Like the knights of Camelot, NGOs are courageous and righteous crusaders that live and breathe the credo, "All for one, and one for all." As such, they acknowledge the worth of every soul is great in the eyes of God.

The actions of NGOs are driven by peace rather than war. They seek to save and improve lives, rather than discard or disrespect them. They seek to uplift and unify humanity by virtuous principles, rather than segregate or divide it by personal agenda or faction groups.

They are team builders and team players that create and protect the virtues and rules of the game.

NGO lives are a testament to charity, selflessness, constant forward motion, continual improvement, and unity. The unique gifts and talents of NGOs, and their commitment and passion in filling the measure of their creation, are the very basis for happiness and joy in this life and the next.

Humble Giants

NGOs are humble giants that diligently seek the will of God and shun personal aggrandizement. You will not find them dancing in the end-zone or calling attention to themselves.

NGOs live passionate, purposeful, and noble lives. They hold themselves personally accountable for their mistakes and shortcomings and are ever-aware of the impact their speech, actions, and influence have on others.

NGOs find their satisfaction, happiness, and joy come from filling the measure of their creation, servitude, and inspiring others to do the same. NGOs bring honor to God, themselves, their loved ones, and their communities. The ripple effect of NGOs and their contributions to the religious, moral, and betterment of humanity are immediate and eternal.

NGO Arenas of Discipline

NGOs today enjoy more arenas for discovery and expression for their unique gifts and talents than any other time or place in history. The venues for expression, the competition, and the level of performance have grown enormously. The press, paparazzi, video networks, and television stations can spotlight newsworthy accomplishments at the speed of light. These pinnacles of expression provide a bandwidth of media promotion, unlike any other time in world history.

Qualities with Distinction

The primary criterion used to select the overachievers you will read about was based on Internet statistics. The second criterion was the individual's ability to make their discipline's dominance to appear E.A.S.I.E.R (Your first acronym! reflecting the disciplines and traits representing the NGO selected).

E represents EMOTION. These NGOs were heralded and lauded for the raw EMOTION they exhibited in achieving their goals or objectives.

A represents ATHLETIC ability. In this category, we will list the top 50 sports based on Internet viewing statistics. Highlighted is the most recognized athlete in the top 15 sports.

S represents SPIRITUALITY. Individuals who emulated a love of God and a concern for others. These purposeful and compassionate spiritual magi devoted their lives to uplifting those around them and perpetuating an eternal perspective.

I represents INTELLIGENCE. These mental giants are recognized for their stratospheric IQs and boundaryless ways of thinking. Some have discovered and propagated new frontiers of research, learning, and understanding. More than just a street name or an epitaph, their contributions furthered the cause of science and have blessed the lives of billions.

E represents EXPLORERS. These are the ones who, using a Star Trek reference, "Boldly Go Where No Man Has Gone Before." These courageous pioneers risked life and limb to discover new frontiers for expansion and colonization. Included in this category are pioneers of discovery, individuals devoted their lives searching for medical cures and inventions to benefit mankind.

Our last letter, R, represents RESILIENCE. These boundless, bounce-back individuals

(BBI) have cultivated within themselves an ability to maintain their identities and direction regardless of their circumstances or the challenges that confront them. Their character, courage, and strength are a byproduct of learning their true identities and purposes at an early age and forging within themselves the commitment to overcome failure, setback, and adversity for the glory of God.

Rock Stars with a Purpose

NGOs can become powerful leaders and their ability to attract loyal followers can be enormous. It is not uncommon for NGOs to draw viewership in the billions.

NGOs are multi-dimensionally gifted. They can be courageous and tenacious in defending and pursuing a worthy cause. Yet, they can also be reserved, non-judgmental, and compassionate toward those who falter, lose their way, or are negatively impacted by the actions of others.

NGOs can be monolithic magnets in attracting individuals who are experiencing personal trials, setbacks, and adversity. To these struggling soldiers, NGOs can be a beacon of hope, a standard for courage, and a model of resilience. They command our attention and inspire us to seek our own unique strengths, giftedness, and purpose.

As you read *The Noble and Great Ones*, may you pause, ponder, and reflect upon the remarkable accomplishments of the individuals mentioned in this book, the challenges they overcame, the unique gifts and talents they discovered early in life, and the degree to which they became legendary in their respective disciplines and filled the measure of their creation. I hope that by reading this book, your desire to uncover your own talents, abilities, and identity will awaken you to your own nobility and greatness.

Living an NGO Life

As you ponder the power, purpose, and influence of the NGOs you will read about, your image, understanding, and appreciation for what it takes to live an NGO life will increase.

In some instances, you may ponder and ask yourself, "Could these gifted ones have done more to bless the lives of others?" Or "Were their efforts and contributions equal to or greater than the accomplishment itself? Did they use the full tank, or was it just a quarter of a tank?"

What more could these gifted ones have done to bless the lives of others? By what standard do we judge them? By what standard do we judge ourselves? Are we qualified to judge anyone? Perhaps we ought to let God be the judge?

Becoming NGO Fit

Once you have finished reading *The Noble and Great Ones*, there will be just three questions remaining to be answered. First, "Am I filling the measure of my creation?" Second, "What changes need I make to do so?" And third, "when should I begin?"

Being "NGO fit" does not come easily. Nor does it come overnight. But it does come to those who strive to know themselves, improve themselves, and give of themselves purposefully and selflessly. The joy we experience in this life is a validation of where we are on the path of filling the measure of our creation. Conversely, the sadness, grief, or unrest we experience in life is a warning when we are not.

I hope that by reading *The Noble and Great Ones*, you will recognize and appreciate the undaunted fortitude and unwavering commitment it takes to become a champion and a ruler within a particular discipline. It is my prayer that, as you learn about the tremendous achievements wrought by these NGOs, the impact they made on their future disciples, and the legacies they left to humanity, you will aspire to seek out your own divinity, nobility, and aptitude for greatness within you.

May we each muster the faith, courage, and commitment within us to discover the laden gifts and talents within us, and in so doing bring newfound purpose to your own life, the lives of others, and to humanity.

It is Not About Proportions

Nobility and greatness cannot and should not be measured by proportion alone. Rather, it should be measured substantively by its impact on the giver and the receiver. Although multitudes can witness nobility and greatness, it is most often seen in small groups and one-on-one close interactions and encounters. We must always remember, "It's Not About Proportions, It's What's in the Glass That Matters Most."

You are the workmanship of God's eternal hands. He created you in His image and likeness. As your creator, He knows you far better than you know yourself. He is mindful of each of us, regardless of race, color, religion, or persuasion. He loves all His children equally. As a child of God, there is divinity within you to change your stance, supplant bad habits, improve your circumstance, and become a new creature. As you learn to align your will with His, you will experience more happiness and joy than you could ever think possible.

Of all the living organisms on earth, humans are the only life form that can further, limit, or reverse their eternal progression. Embracing change, overcoming trials and adversity, and maintaining a path of forward motion with continual improvement is requisite to filling the measure of your creation and living a life of nobility and greatness.

Nobility by Nature

By placing nobility first, our thoughts, deeds, and actions become ethically and morally weighed, measured, and executed by our conscience – that moral compass within us all.

Two acronyms can influence the outcome of our race in life the most. Our conscious decision to embrace one over the other will make the difference between joy and happiness. One acronym is "Life Giving" and the other is "Life Taking."

The first one can lead us toward Life Eternal, build self-confidence, and grow trust in God. It can strengthen faith, confidence, and purpose in our lives. Those that embrace its life-giving words have the ability to rise above their trials and afflictions. The Acronym is O.P.T.I.M.I.S.M.

> O represents Openness. Optimists embrace, encourage, and evoke open and authentic dialogue. They are open to change. They are open to new ideas, new possibilities, and new opportunities.

> P represents Prayer. Optimists use prayer to call upon the powers of heaven for inspiration, direction, and strength. They maintain a prayer in their hearts for those that suffer emotionally, physically, or spiritually.

> T represents Teachable. As a rule, optimists make intelligent, well-informed, and guided decisions. They rely on the advice of mentors and respect the advice of others. Optimists thrive on growing knowledge and wisdom that

inspire faith and a fresh perspective. They applaud the successes of others and encourage those that strive for self-improvement.

I represents Intelligence. The quality has three primary facets. First, Intelligence refers to the light of truth, a spiritual matter that gives life and light to all things. Second, Intelligence may also refer to our spiritual nature in the premortal world. Third, the scriptures mention intelligence as a spirit element or matter in the universe that has always existed. We will spend more time on this subject in the chapter *The Intellectual Rulers.*

M represents magnify, meaning to make something look larger than it is. Those who emulate positivity, or a "can-do attitude," attract those seeking the same. Mary Lou Retton, the first American woman to win the all-around gold medal at the Olympics, believes, "Optimism is a happiness magnet, if you stay positive, good things and good people will be drawn to you."

This second letter "I" represents Integrity. Optimists consistently do what is right and let the consequences follow. They are trustworthy, dependable, and obedient to the mind and will of God. They value God's mind and will above themselves and use their personal inspiration to determine His will versus the opinion of others.

S represents Sustainability. Optimists stay the course to their objectives and reach their goals more frequently than do naysayers.

The final "M" represents Multiply. Optimists

seek to increase in stature and favor with God and man. They believe in themselves and strive to multiply and magnify the unique talents within them. They use most of their time to bless the lives of others. Optimists, by their very presence, draw the attention and interest of others. They encourage, lift, inspire, and attract discipleship quickly. Optimism brings light, life, and raises the level of our consciousness.

Optimists focus their efforts and energy on things they have control over and pray for strength to endure, the patience to understand, and in time to accept, understand, and embrace life-changing events that are beyond their control.

Optimists consistently seek opportunities to share their wisdom with others. They embrace every opportunity to reason, communicate, and express themselves directly, indirectly, and robustly. They are passionate about discovering, embracing, and defending the truth. They are quick to share their life experiences and the lessons they have learned and do so openly, thoughtfully, and passionately.

Optimists can draw listeners, followers, and disciples overnight. They innately take a stand on principles and moral issues rather than remain neutral and watch others act. Because they let their light shine, they often draw opponents and antagonists and sometimes infuriate special interest supporters. NGOs unceasingly search for new ideas, new possibilities, and new opportunities for personal improvement and helping others.

Optimists pray to see and understand the Bigger Picture. They generally possess more pieces of the puzzle to make an accurate assessment, yet they are humble enough to rely on inspiration from above. They pray frequently with great earnest to find the right piece.

Pessimism is the dark and antithesis side of Optimism. Its roots originate from Lucifer, the Prince of Darkness, and the master of identity theft. He uses our trials, disappointments, and setbacks to lower our self-esteem, acquiesce in stinking thinking, and embrace fear, apathy, and doubt. Those who choose to live a pessimistic life are in direct opposition to their purpose in coming here. Pessimists are: Prideful, Exclusionary, Self-absorbed, Self-Righteous, Ignorant, Maladjusted, Insensitive, Sad, and operate in a state of Malaise.

Pessimists live unhappy and unfulfilling lives. They place great emphasis on the proportions in their glass rather than the substance inside the glass. They have given up on whatever dreams they may have had, whatever joy they may have experienced, and whatever reward they may have received.

Pessimists exchange fight for flight, faith for fear, and hope for despair. Pessimists would rather defend non-ability than to over-extend themselves in pursuit of true nobility. They would rather over-indulge themselves in tenderloins than to gird up their loins in quest of a worthy crusade. Generally speaking, most pessimists would rather wallow in the pit of self-pity and defeat rather than press forward and win the victory.

Those that choose to embrace pessimism are in direct opposition to their purpose in coming here.

Pessimism is fertile ground for the cultivation of fear, apathy, and doubt (FAD). Another acronym associated with pessimism is D.E.S.P.A.I.R. (Depression, Envy, Self-Righteousness, Pride, Anger, Ignorance, and Retaliation, aka Revenge).

These two acronyms represent the most frequently used fiery darts of the adversary and are the foundation upon which we can be robbed of our true identity, nobility, and aptitude for greatness. Our ability to rise above these soul-eroding thoughts is requisite to our journey here in mortality.

A Purposeful Life

The choices you made before your mortal birth are a testament to the nobility and greatness within you. You knew the vicissitudes of earth life, the adversities, trials, and temptations of mortality before coming here. It was the love you felt toward your Father in Heaven, your desire to please him and be more like him, which was the basis for your valiancy and courage in coming here.

It must have been exciting, and perhaps a bit daunting, as the time of your arrival drew near. The overall emotion you felt about coming here was joy. As the book of Job records, we shouted for joy for having a chance in coming here. (Job 38:7)

It is the reacquaintance, realignment, and recognition of your identity that can fuel your passions, raise your commitment levels, and impel you to overcome perceived weaknesses, shortcomings, and setbacks.

The purpose for coming here is to prove ourselves, fulfill the measure of our creation, and have joy. The successes we have along this path of discovery, the awakening experience, and the degree to which we serve others will have the greatest impact on our attitude, altitude, and amplitude in life.

The gifts and talents that make you unique, whether recognized or not yet discovered, are a part of your identity. They can be a tremendous benefit in fostering self-esteem, inspiring personal improvement, and overcoming trials and adversity. However, this is not the primary reason for which they were bestowed. These blessed talents are given to lift, inspire, and bless the lives of God's children, especially those within your own family and among your circles of influence. Your development, eternal progression, and eventual reward in heaven will be in direct proportion to the way you magnified your gifts and talents for the benefit of others while filling the measure of your creation.

The Role of Personal Adversity

Our ability to overcome trials, afflictions, and adversity in this life is one of the greatest legacies we can bequest upon our descendants. Enduring trials can strengthen us, our loved ones, and our posterity.

Adversity is a schoolmaster for empathy that can foster compassion within us to serve others that suffer. Trials can draw us closer to our Father in heaven as we rely on His help and strength to deliver us or, if it be His will, to sustain us through the adversity we are experiencing. Adversity can improve prayer and Increase the frequency of meaningful scripture study.

The greater the dilemma and conflict, the greater the need for heavenly help from above. If you have not yet experienced pain, suffering, or trials in your life, buckle up your seat belt. They surely will come; they are one of the primary reasons you are here. Seven trial-less days makes one weak. As the Apostle Paul, who was well acquainted with trials, testified to the saints in Corinth, "When I am weak, then am I strong." (2 Corinthians 12:10)

These are qualities of the Great and Noble Ones. They reflect confidence in making decisions and attract loyal followers by their accomplishments. Although they recognize their limitations, they know that with God's help and intervention all things are possible. The more they and we can acknowledge the Father's intervention in our lives, the more thankful, dependent, and loyal we can become in serving and carrying out His will.

Progression and change is the very essence of why we came here. Whether positively or negatively perceived, our experiences in this life add up to at least four things; knowledge, wisdom, understanding, and empathy. The daily choices we make and the habits we form in this life build our character, forge our perspective, and reveal our identity. Those that recognize and magnify their gifts and talents early in life often enjoy greater success in this life and eternal rewards in the life to come.

NGOs excel mentally, emotionally, physically, and spiritually because they often discover and develop their gifts and talents early in life. The effort they put forth, the level of achievement they attain, and the resiliency they exhibit during adversity and defeat is an inspiration and an invitation to seek out our own talents, opportunities, and possibilities.

The individuals you will read about in this book achieved tremendous success in the disciplines in which they performed. Their capability, commitment, and indomitable spirit within them, combined with their tenacity, resiliency, and a relentless drive to stay the course and go the distance until the goal was attained, are the qualities that elevated their reputations to legendary proportions. These exceptional individuals excelled in seemingly impossible circumstances and against highly improbable odds.

John A. Shedd wrote, "A ship is safe in harbor, but that's not what ships are for." There is no progression in complacency, no wisdom in ignorance, and no joy in apathy. Our lives are fueled by purpose, and purpose is why we are here!

You are not, nor were you ever born to be an "Average Joe." A comfort zone is a small prison for inmates with mistaken identities, and there are no get out of jail for free cards or collect $200 rewards for passing go.

Nobility and greatness is within you. Discover it, cultivate it, and share it to bless the lives of others. Get out there, fill the measure of your creation, become the person you were meant to be, and in so doing, change the world around you. You were meant to embark upon this journey. You are here at this exact moment in time for a specific purpose. The barometer that you are fulfilling that purpose is Joy.

Your Un-comparable-ness

It is human nature to compare ourselves with others.

Before a race begins, we may see a runner that we would deem unfit to compete, who then causes us to marvel as he or she miraculously and seemingly effortlessly crosses the finish line well before we do. We may then compare our performance to theirs, criticizing ourselves for our shortcomings and poor performance. You may be a competitive golfer who plays a round at scratch, then the following week struggles to reach bogie.

The correction rarely ever comes by pushing harder, but rather by returning to fundamentals and best practices. This is the fastest way to improve performance.

It is always important to remember that whatever the challenge we may face in life, our performance is rarely a representation of the truth, but rather a reflection of our spiritual, mental, and physical preparation.

Maintaining a positive inner dialogue in moments of uncertainty can make the difference between standing tall, performance, and success in life. Optimism ingrains a positive pattern that becomes a pathway and protection for managing future trials and adversity. Never allow pessimism to diminish your self-worth, purpose, or progression in life.

In *The Noble and Great Ones*, we will expand on virtues that shape nobility in the bearer and the emotional, physical, and mental preparation it takes to achieve remarkable results.

We can all feel somewhat insecure when we compete with someone who exhibits superior athleticism, creativity, or intellect. It is not uncommon to ponder why another is so gifted, blessed, or whose abilities and achievements are significantly more abundant than our own. Although these thoughts and feelings may be common, when we allow another's ability and success to cause us to question or doubt our self-worth, talent, and ability, we degrade our divine ancestry, inheritance, and potential for nobility and greatness. The reward of such thinking is a regressive journey leading downward and the restrictive emotions that accompany such a fall.

The impact of FAD in our lives can have a far greater negative influence on our forward progression than the fads of fashion. It is far easier to change an outfit than to change habits and one's self-image. The FAD we will discuss, and the damage these negative influences can have in our lives, may reach into the eternities. FAD is the first indicator a victim is falling toward D.E.S.P.A.I.R.

When we measure our self-worth and capability by volume, surplus, or deficiency when observing the performance and accomplishments of another, we devalue and dismiss our own uniqueness and possibilities. It is deceiving and sinful to associate what we have with who we are; or what we can or cannot do with what we can or cannot become. Those who appear to have it all are often those who have the least, and those with the least are usually the most grateful and happy for what they have. As we sojourn through life, we must value what is inside our glass rather than what is in someone else's glass.

As a son or daughter of God, it is unnatural and contrary to your purpose in coming here to entertain thoughts of inferiority or to depreciate the value or potential for greatness within you. By focusing on quantity and proportions versus quality and substance, we degrade the very nature of who we are and whence we came. Our individual worth will not be measured by how far, how long, or how fast we can run. It will be measured by our contributions and the impact we make in our marriages, with our children, and for our communities.

The Two Realities of Life

We must come to terms with two realities in this life if we are to reduce stress and live happily. The first reality is there are things we CAN CONTROL. The second reality is there are things we CANNOT CONTROL. The things we can control include our thoughts, choices, and the consequences thereof.

In other words, the things we have control over are things related to agency and our freedom to choose. Examples of things we cannot control are illness, birth gender, nationality, biological parents, and time. We have agency in thought to dwell on one reality or the other. But we cannot dwell on both since our minds are designed to entertain one thought at a time. Choose wisely, for there is an opportunity cost that comes with each.

In choosing to focus on things within our control, we improve attitude, optimism, faith, possibilities, gratitude, perseverance, potential, and are more apt to fulfill the measure of our creation. The benefit of focusing our thoughts on controllable things is there is no room or time left to entertain pity parties, disappointment, frustration, sorrow, cynicism, pessimism, unfulfillment, and despair. By choosing to dwell on things beyond our control, we forego any chance for nobility and greatness within ourselves. The choice is entirely ours.

Neverland, a Place of Possibilities

The Pan Principle is real. As you reacquaint yourself with your unique identity, the things that seemed difficult or even impossible will dissipate, and it will become easier to align your will with that of your Heavenly Father. As your true self begins to emerge, you will reach a clearing in which all things are possible. The divinity within you will impel you to overcome hurdles and setbacks and the adventure of a lifetime will begin.

Living the life of an NGO is simply living the life you were meant to live and filling the measure of which you were born. As you so live, others will be encouraged and inspired to test their own limitations and overcome their own perceived shortcomings, setbacks, or failures. Your example and encouragement will inspire others to replace pessimism with optimism, despair with hope, and doubt with possibilities.

As you continue along this path of fulfilling the measure of your creation, you will eventually reach a clearing where all things are possible. Your life will become purposefully driven and reflect the divine heritage from which you were born. In the words of Eric Little, "I believe God made me for a purpose, but he also made me fast. And when I run, I feel His pleasure."

May you discover and unleash the nobility and greatness within you for the glory of God, the betterment of self, and to bless your fellowman. May we exchange our erroneous and false inhibitions, incarcerating impressions of self-limitations, and inferiority with a true image of our divine heritage and divine potential. May you bless countless lives along the way and embrace the credo that "It's not about proportions, it's what's in the glass that matters most."

May you find and develop the divine substance of who you are and experience more joy and fulfillment than you have ever imagined or experienced before. There is nobility and greatness within you, now go and find it!

CHAPTER 2

The Rules, Tools, and the Playing Field

I t was in a premortal existence that you and I were first weighed, measured, and found worthy to live here in mortality.

What are the common attributes found in Great and Noble Ones?

First, regardless of proportions, they acknowledge and are grateful to God for what fills their glasses. They seem to recognize their unique gifts and experience confidence early. Regardless of the personal trials encountered, the adversities endured, or the challenges or setbacks faced along their personal journeys, they know who they are, from whence they came, and where they are going. The spiritual identity they possess remains intact no matter what issues they are called to endure.

Second, they have a pure love of God and a genuine concern for the welfare of others. They live by and for the "all for one, and one for all" creed. They continually strive to lift and inspire others toward godliness and respect for all God's children, both individually and collectively. Faith, hope, love, and charity are the essence of the fuel that passionately and endlessly propels them.

Third, they convert their adjectives to adverbs, emulating and magnifying their gifts. The attributes that define them are found in all NGOs and can be sunned up in a single word: O.P.T.I.M.I.S.T.I.C. NGOs are Overly Achieving, Passionately Driven, Talentedly Laden, Intensely Persistent, Mentally Superior, Idealistically Rooted, Spiritually Minded, Tenaciously Advocating, Insightfully Gifted, and Compassionately Boundaryless.

NGO character traits reflect high moral values, lofty ideals, and an innate sense of humanity toward their fellow man.

Noble and Great Qualities Personified

Throughout history, there have been countless individuals who have unarguably exhibited the qualities of nobility and greatness. These individuals are often identified by the adjectives they personified. A few familiar examples of such individuals, and the adjectives by which they were known, include Abraham Lincoln, Job, and Solomon.

Honest Abe Lincoln - Honest Abe (referring to Abraham Lincoln) was arguably one of the greatest presidents in American History. His mother, Mary Todd, once described her son Abe as being almost monomaniac in the subject of honesty. As a young store clerk in New Salem, Illinois, when realizing he had shortchanged a customer, even by just a few pennies, he would close the shop and travel regardless of the distance to the affected party and deliver them the correct change.

Lincoln was frequently called upon to act as a judge and mediator because of his honesty. Robert Rutledge, who lived in New Salem once remarked, "Lincoln's judgment was final...people relied implicitly upon his honesty, integrity, and impartiality." Before he entered the legal profession, he admitted that his future profession was known for its dishonesty. His advice to those entering this practice was, "Resolve to be honest at all events; and if in your judgment, you cannot be an honest lawyer, resolve to be honest without being a lawyer. Choose some other occupation, rather than one in the choosing of which you do, in advance, consent to be a knave." In other words, be true to yourself and those you represent.

It is deplorable that such honesty and integrity in today's politics and presidential elections that candidates and society in general, must choose the "lesser of evils" as their preferred candidate for the highest office in America. Honesty and integrity in our selection process today carries little to no merit on election day. The noble qualities of nobility that our Founding Fathers held so dear, and that Americans once heralded and even demanded of government officials, is no longer a requirement. In fact, in some instances, it is even overlooked and replaced by rhetoric and ratings.

Thorns and Thistles Along the Way

Personal trials, adversity, and opposition in life are the three key essential ingredients for self-realization, self-improvement, and self-mastery.

Adversity is necessary for our eternal progression and indispensable in filling the measure of our creation. If you have not yet faced or been required to endure a significant trial or adversity, get ready. They are coming. It is how we endure our earthly trials and adversities that testifies to our submission to the will of God and our commitment to endure all things for His glory.

As we stay the course amidst our trials and burdens, maintaining faith and submitting to the will of the Father, we bear witness to others that we are in submission to God's will and for His glory and honor, rather than for our own self servitude and personal gain. This passion and strength of character is the hallmark quality of the NGO. It is what inspires godliness, reveals strength of character, and opens the portals of humility and gratitude. As the NGO fills the measure of their creation, freedom, liberty, and the pursuit of justice are preserved, and Satan's powers are dispelled.

A Word on Humility

Although NGOs have a greater calling and capacity for nobility and greatness, it does not mean they will automatically reach world status or recognition. There are NGOs among us who may prefer to maintain a lower profile void of public fanfare. These humble giants may accomplish heroic acts and deeds, yet prefer to remain anonymous and incognito rather than receive reward, recognition, or public acclaim. The humility they exhibit is a common quality found in NGOs. We will introduce these unique individuals in the chapter *The Unsung Heroes.*

Whether you are an atheist, agnostic, or a believer. Whether you follow Eastern or Western religion, kick with your right or left foot (an expression I learned while living in Northern Ireland in 1977, denoting whether you are a Catholic or a Protestant), nobility and greatness are within you.

It is a defining feature that separates the apathetic person from the passionate overachiever, the pessimist from the optimist, the average from the extraordinary. Greatness is genderless, non-denominational, colorless, and impartial to individual interpretation. Greatness can be found at any time, in any instance or circumstance, and in any location within or without our known universe.

Greatness Throughout History

Acts of greatness were preserved in clay tablets dating back to the 7th century BC. With the dawning of publishing in the mid-1400s with the Guttenberg Bible, mass production publications spread these stories. Access to greatness has exploded in the past century. Through the proliferation of the radio, television, and the Internet, greatness can now be accessed almost instantaneously.

The potential for greatness began before our mortal birth. It was foreordained in heaven and heralded by angels. It has been witnessed by wise men and can be seen, to varying degrees, within every individual physically born into this plane of existence known as mortality.

True greatness is an eternal gift from an all-knowing, infinitely loving God to His spiritual sons and daughters. The workmanship of His hands can be seen upon every infant born upon this earth. Unfortunately, potential provides no guarantee for success. It is not a predestined trait; rather, it is a gift from an all-knowing, all-powerful, infinitely compassionate Father in Heaven who gave His Only Begotten Son, chosen and foreordained to become the savior and redeemer of all mankind.

Our success will grow as we learn to love God, our fellow man, and exercise our agency in a manner that pleases Him. Our reward will be the joy we experience in this life and the mansion prepared for us into the eternities.

Several requirements must exist to acknowledge and herald greatness. The first requirement is Purpose. The act must have a worthy objective or end goal. For example, in an era where women were regularly seen as inferior on many fronts, Amelia Earhart became an icon of courage and inner strength through her early childhood experiences. Her greatness remains an inspiration, a beacon of hope, and an ensign to us all. Her great message is that if your purpose, cause, and actions resonate with others, are channeled and ingrained within you, and your desire is strong enough, you can achieve almost anything. Earhart was only the 16th woman to earn a pilot's license. In 1928, she was the first woman to fly across the Atlantic Ocean. Later she became the first person to fly over both the Atlantic and Pacific oceans.

The second requirement is Magnitude, meaning the act or deed must raise the bar by some degree, establishing a new standard for excellence and drawing others to seek out their own unique gifts and talents. Greatness breeds individual self-assessment and self-realization. It fuels competition and motivates self-discovery and self-improvement. This principle has been the underlying bedrock of marketing success for decades. Examples include the slogan "Be All That You Can Be," used by the U.S. Army for 20 years. "Be Like Mike" was a Gatorade slogan used in Michael Jordan ads that aired for 23 years, matching Jordan's jersey number. A coincidence? I think not.

The third requirement is that greatness must create Loyalty. To this day, there are avid fans who will endure discomfort, adversity, and a bit of insanity to defend and support an individual, cause, or achievement.

Finally, the fourth element of greatness is Retell-ability, meaning the act or accomplishment inspires the recipient to tell the story to others. Greatness creates a buzz, inspires others, shapes thought, opinions, and action. Greatness demands self-assessment and action. It should inspire a change of action and purpose.

Self-Serve Greatness

Unfortunately, as previously discussed, Greatness, unlike Nobility, can (and often does) set aside its moral compass. In doing so, it seeks its own gain and exalts its bearer beyond personal ethics, legal responsibilities, and respect of others. Its boundary-less potential can be perpetuated through undisciplined behavior, pride, and sheer arrogance.

Greatness in this form can be self-serving, self-gratifying, self-perpetuating, and entirely self-destructive. Such selfish behavior has been witnessed in every corner of the globe, at any point in history, and, as ancient scripture reveals, before the foundation of this earth was laid.

Steroids and drug enhancements may bear statistical fruit, but at what cost? At what price does an athlete choose to exchange his or her own integrity for the thrill of victory and the fame that follows? At what point do we understand the subject or disciplinary commitment to ace the test without seeking an easy alternative?

At what point does an NGO throw in the towel and retreat to the comfort and security of lowered expectations and self-preservation?

How should an NGO react to pain, suffering, and adversity? Are they defeated by it, or do they use it as a springboard in cultivating divine virtues within themselves, such as nobility, patience, longsuffering endurance, and wisdom?

Becoming an NGO

In *The Noble and Great Ones*, we will identify and expand upon the common ingredients that personify all NGOs. These qualities foster their reservoir of giftedness and ignite the driving forces within them to overcome obstacles, excel, and seek the powers of heaven. We will discuss from where this desire and indomitable spirit to press forward and keep trying comes. We will identify the common denominator that lifts the average person beyond mediocrity's comfort to reach for the summit of superiority or pinnacle of humanitarianism. In the chapters ahead, we will seek to answers these and other important questions to understand further the role these unique individuals play in society.

The Noble and Great Ones identifies and personifies innate qualities that are exhibited within NGOs. These traits are often recognized early in life. They have a direct bearing on an individual's aptitude and altitude to press forward, reaching beyond perceived personal weakness until they realize their full potential, filling the measure of their creation. To an NGO, reveling in his or her success is but a fleeting moment. There are still mountains to climb, oceans to cross, and the world is still ripe for conquering. An NGO's motivation is not found in arriving at the finish line, but rather in the journey itself and the lives blessed along the way. The motivating factor in all instances is how did we impact the lives of others?

The thoughts, actions, and accomplishments of the NGO will always be in alignment with the humanitarian needs of society. NGOs seem to know earlier than others who they are, from whence their unique talents came, and where they are heading. They live purpose-driven lives inspiring others to do the same. They are often voraciously driven and competitive with themselves. The fire in their belly that propels them forward is inextinguishable.

Noble and Great Ones may be revered for their remarkable athleticism or their uncanny intellect. Some will be remembered for their exceptional oratory skills, others for the sheer passion and emotional tenacity in fighting for a worthy cause. And some will be remembered for possessing a seemingly endless reservoir of spiritual insight, sound judgment, and pure wisdom.

Greatness, though it may lead to fame and fortune, does not in itself guarantee Nobleness. Greatness may even be self-serving and diabolically opposed to Nobility. Throughout history, many individuals have achieved great accomplishments while remaining seemingly oblivious to the trail of destruction they were causing.

Give Credit Where and When Credit is Due

It is common today for a champion to attain an extraordinary feat and fail to give credit to others who were instrumental in laying the foundation for their accomplishment in the first place. The fruit of these great ones will wither one day and die on the vine of their own self-aggrandizement. The legendary greatness they may have achieved will become a distant figment of their imagination.

Rather than being an inspiration to humanity through self-redeeming acts of honesty, generosity, humility, and morality, the accomplishments of these glory hogs will soon be forgotten. Any greatness they may have achieved will be remembered by how it was attained, rather than the merits of the individuals themselves.

Greatness, when void of nobility, will always leave the individual unfulfilled and restricted in their eternal progression. Although a person may accomplish a great feat, if it only benefits himself or herself the benefit is meaningless. Without nobility as the motivating force, no accomplishment will ever be self-redeeming or praiseworthy. The misuse of personal agency and giftedness can have dire consequences. It can estrange us from the true source of all giftedness and result in personal accountability and self-degradation. Greatness unbridled by nobility can send the bearer on a downward slope leading to darkness and despair.

The Fall of Pessimism

Pessimists live unhappy and unfulfilling lives.

They place great emphasis on the proportions in their glasses rather than the substance inside the glass. They have given up on whatever dreams they may have had, whatever joy they may have experienced, and whatever reward they may have received.

They exchange fight for flight, faith for fear, possibility for improbability, and nobility for no-ability. They would rather give up than live up to the expectations of others. If given a choice between wallowing in a mire of self-pity and apathy, versus pressing forward and winning the victory, they will choose the path of least resistance rather than risk failure.

By contrast, nobility is a chosen path that leads the bearer upward toward the well of thanksgiving, the beacon of accomplishment, and the joy in humanity found in reaching one's true potential. Nobility, by virtue itself, can lift humanity to a higher plane of thought and meaningful purpose.

The Noble and Great Ones are powerful leaders with tremendous influence in igniting meaningful change in others. They typically live by lofty standards, command respect, and some may even gain worldwide recognition. NGOs shun idleness. They maintain elevated levels of energy, and they possess an intensity and passion for extending themselves above human restraints and personal weakness or insecurities.

NGOs aspire to a loftier state of being, to improve current personal circumstances, to stretch abilities, and discover untapped talents from within themselves.

Signs of a Noble and Great One's divinity and purpose are often manifest at birth, but are more commonly detectable in adolescence and early adulthood. Nobility and Greatness progress throughout one's lifetime, as the Noble and Great Ones realize their unique talents. This pushes them beyond personal limitations to the threshold of identity and meaningful purpose. Greatness may not reflect Nobility, but Nobility will always reflect Greatness.

The Noble and Great Ones was written to spotlight individuals who fulfill the definition of a Noble and Great One. There are three primary purposes for this book. First, to recognize and appreciate the Noble and Great Ones who have influenced our lives and positively impacted society. Second, to evoke within the reader curiosity to seek and awaken their own unique gifts, talents, and abilities that may lay dormant within them, but that are never-the-less an essential part of their identity. Third, to instill within the reader a desire to stay the course in developing their unique gifts, passing beyond perceived human barriers and restrictions, acknowledging the source of their divine potential, and sharing these gifts for the betterment of society and world humanity.

Thus, the role of *The Noble and Great Ones* is to encourage, motivate, inspire, and lift others to realize their true potential and fulfill their purpose here in mortality. Whether you are a Millennial, Gen-X, Baby Boomer, or Traditionalist, you have likely been influenced by the examples, attributes, and accomplishments of others. It is also likely some of their achievements have already inspired and motivated you to press forward beyond your fears, personal insecurities, and judgments of others to access your inner mental, physical, spiritual, or emotional strength. Or perhaps these have motivated or inspired you to reach a summit of personal achievement and jubilant satisfaction despite naysayers and cynical efforts to dissuade you.

The discovery of identity and attainment of our divine potential is innate. The indication that we are on the right path toward fulfilling the measure of our creation can be described in one word: Joy.

Simply put, when we are on the correct path of fulfilling our individual destinies, when we feel jubilant, triumphant, happy, exhilarated, euphoric, elated, and blissful, these emotions are comprised in the word joy. Hope then becomes an actual force for personal improvement.

Conversely, when we are on the wrong path, we experience negative emotions that erode our sense of identity and crush our divine potential. These counterfeit feelings are the antithesis of godliness. They are the fiery darts of Satan delivered with laser-like accuracy at the hearts of the sons and daughters of God.

The Fall of Despair

These devious weapons were at the heart of Lucifer's expulsion from heaven and can be encompassed in a single word and objective, D.E.S.P.A.I.R.:

> Depression (Anger turned inward.)
>
> Envy (A sense of entitlement based on low self-esteem, perpetuated by ingratitude.)
>
> Self-righteousness (Thinking you are more holy or better than another.)

Pride (Exalting oneself, placing your value, worth, or ability above another person.)

Apathy (You have given up on personal improvement or making a meaningful difference.) Apathy arises from unfulfilled expectations; things did not happen the way that you anticipated or expected them to happen. Apathy is, in one sense, giving up on your noble birthright because you choose your own path rather than the path God wants you to follow.

Ignorance (Stinking thinking.) Judging others and your own circumstances without having all the facts. A belief that your attitude and outlook are the fault of someone else, such as playing the victim role and wrongly placing accountability on someone else.

Resentment (Holding a grudge against an individual or certain outcome or harboring ill feelings is contrary to the principle of forgiveness and self-condemning.)

These seven destructive character traits of despair are the adversary's arsenal skillfully aimed at our weakest parts. Just as the arrow that pierced the heal of the invincible Achilles, despair is one of Satan's most lethal weapons he uses when we are at our lowest.

Despair can compromise identity and drag its victim down a dark path that is contrary to fulfilling the measure of our creation and experiencing any semblance of happiness or joy. The fruits in sustaining such a path are disappointment, discouragement, disillusionment, desperation, and eventual damnation (or inability to progress). Hope then turns to hopelessness, faith turns to faithlessness, and the divine potential of what could and may have been is eventually supplanted by cannot and feeling incapable of finding a way out of a situation.

During times of doubt, discouragement, and uncertainty, may we always remember, "it's not about proportions, it's what's in the glass that matters most." The degree of optimism or pessimism we maintain in times of difficulty directly reflects what side of the fence we have chosen to plant our flag. The re-acquainting of our premortal identity can come to each of us as we acknowledge the source of whence we came, why we are here, and where we are heading.

Maintaining that perspective is fueled by hope and evidenced by joy. This state of mind can lift our sense of self-worth above mortal restrictions and perceived shortcomings to touch the heavens. In the words of the poet William Wadsworth, we were born, "Not in entire forgetfulness, and not in utter nakedness, but trailing clouds of glory do we come, from God, who is our home."

The sad reality is that most of us will live our lives without reaching the full measure of our creation and or recognizing the divine potential within us. However, just because one's name and accomplishments are not carved in the annals of history, or broadcast on national television, does not mean they have failed to live a Noble and Great life. There are countless numbers of headstones worldwide that bear the names of remarkable people who lived extraordinary lives but whose life experiences came and went with little publicity or fanfare. These individuals were unarguably noble and great by all standards of the words. However, by their own humility or perhaps divine intervention, they lived and died with almost no recognition or fanfare. Several of these individuals will be highlighted ahead in the chapter *Unsung Hereos*.

I hope that as you read *The Noble and Great Ones,* your appreciation will increase toward those individuals that walked the walk in this life, pressing themselves beyond mental, physical, spiritual, and emotional boundaries and barriers. In sacrificing their time, talents, and their very lives, they created a basecamp or starting point for others to build upon. May our climb be like theirs as we strive to reach our personal summits of growth and rise above our mortal restraints. May we live our lives in our circles of influence in such a way that inspires and lifts others to do the same.

My desire is that by recognizing the sacrifices, endurance, achievements, and legacies of these Noble and Great Ones, your interest in exploring your own mental, physical, emotional, and spiritual strength will increase. I hope your own curiosity will lead you to discover the untapped reservoir of gifts and talents within yourself; once you realize your identity, the bands that once bound you will fade and disappear. Your giftedness is divine and the purpose for your sojourn here on earth is to progress in reaching your true potential and blessing the lives of others.

Your purpose here on earth will be revealed as you stretch beyond your false perceptions and inhibitions, cultivate the dormant greatness and nobility within you, and remain steadfast in further developing the divine qualities that were forged within you before the dawn of mankind. As you do so, you will be a light to others in inspiring them to do the same. Your reward will be a sense of happiness and fulfillment, unlike any you have experienced before. May we each come to realize our true purpose in this life to serve and bless the lives of others through gifts we have been given. That is the requisite and hallmark of a Noble and Great One.

The Noble and Great Ones was written for all people, present and future, for every race, color, and creed. It is for every atheist, agnostic, and believer as a witness that there is a God in Heaven who created us all in His image and who fashioned this earth and gave man and woman dominion over it.

CHAPTER 3

Making It Look "Easier" Than It Really Is

The aptitude for domination was pre-determined and foreordained before our mortal birth. Yet, the inclination, provocation, and realization of one's calling, although it comes by way of divine origin, is still subject to personal agency. It is also subject to man's fallibility in recognizing the opposing forces of the adversary and acquiescing his will contrary to the will of God.

The desire to improve one's self is central to the plan of salvation and exaltation. It is a yearning and desire deep within our souls that drives an NGO to improve oneself and the lives of others.

Rulership began in the pre-mortal world of spirits. It is perceived by the Light of Christ within us all and maintained through acts of nobility and by filling the measure of our creation.

Rulership increases or decreases by every thought we entertain, every decision we make, and every consequence thereof. The refining journey in becoming a great ruler is without beginning or end. It will continue throughout the eternities.

Who can deny the wonderment of an infant at the moment of birth as he or she begins to study and understand the world around them? It accelerates as the infant becomes a toddler and learns how to crawl from one place to another. It flourishes when the infant leaves the fetal position, stands tall, and excitedly learns to walk. As the toddler sees their parents walking, they naturally desire to walk themselves.

Before long, walking is not nearly enough as the child shifts gears to a higher RPM and learns to run. At that point, the infant's personality, purpose, and possibilities are in full bloom, and they find themselves at a crossroad of confidence where all things are possible.

This journey from the fetal position to upright mobility is without argument the most impressionable years in a child's life. The bond between a mother and child during the first six years of the child's life is critical for their self-worth, sense of wellbeing, and sense of security.

When the maternal and paternal bond is strong between the parents and the child, their sense of security grows, affording them the confidence and courage to meet challenges with a healthy perspective and maintain progress. In such an environment, the child can extend their boundaries and begin to recognize their unique abilities.

Experiencing impressions, discovery, and self-mastery broadens the landscape before them and fuels wonderment, imagination, and purpose. This forward motion and progression, coupled with attributes of divinity, provide the strength and courage to leave the nest and become contributing members of society.

Those parents who teach their toddlers and adolescents dependence on God, and one another, increase the odds that their children will attain self-mastery, make good choices, and contribute to society. Children with increased faith that a loving Father in Heaven is watching over them, and is mindful of their struggles and disappointments, are far more prepared to embrace the unexpected changes and overcome the vicissitudes of life and the challenges that eventually come to us all.

A healthy home learning environment teaches children humility, respect, honor, and gratitude for earthly and heavenly parents. Parents who emulate nobility in the home lay a foundation for their children's aptitude for future greatness.

Unfortunately, only a select few of us are born into homes that effectively teach, emulate, and foster rulership. For most of us, our daily actions, commitments, and time spent on trivial pursuits are consistently contrary to our divine nature. All too often, we live below our royal heritage of whence we came and who we are capable of becoming.

Although a ruler may be destined for greatness, he or she becomes as such, line upon line, precept upon precept, until their role in society becomes clear to them. Once the NGO acknowledges their nobility and bandwidth for greatness, he or she will innately and instinctively extend themselves willingly, compassionately, and purposefully for the benefit of humanity.

NGOs will Grow Exponentially in the Future

NGOs today have a built-in marketing platform like none other in history. Since Mark Zuckerberg launched Facebook in his Harvard dorm room on February 4, 2004, his customer base has exploded to 1.3 billion active

Facebook users, with 82 percent coming from outside the U.S. and Canada. Twitter boasts 270 million active users that send 500 million tweets per day. Four billion videos are viewed daily on YouTube (that equals 46,296 per second) and 60 million photos are uploaded daily on Instagram.

The boundless reach of the Internet and television broadcasts provides instant access with the click of a mouse or a tap of a finger. Voice-enabled interfaces (VEI) now make it simple enough to ask and receive instantaneously; just ask Siri, Ling-Dong-L, or Alexa and see what they have to say on the subject. Social media has evolved from a fad into a mainstream phenomenon that has triggered a paradigm shift in how the world operates and communicates.

Access to apps and today's digital technology have empowered individuals to voice their opinions, address current events, and share content of every kind on numerous devices in ways no one could have imagined before the advent of the wireless web, personal digital assistants (PDAs), and apps that can instantaneously deliver to the end-user the information they seek.

What was once local news that took days, months, and, in some cases, years to perpetuate can now be transferred and propagated globally with the click of a mouse or tap of a key on your cell phone or mobile device.

Politics, news, and business are now global. Data is exploding exponentially. 90% of the data found on the Internet today was added in the last two years. It is staggering to consider the amount of data that will be available to our younger generation as they become more independent and self-sufficient.

In today's world, recognition, acclaim, and stardom can be digitally transmitted in a nanosecond. Those who rule and dominate in their disciplines can become stars overnight or branded as criminals in mere seconds.

Although NGOs may acknowledge their spotlight for a small moment, it is their insatiable appetite for spiritual evolution and self-mastery that impels them to perpetually raise their personal bars of achievement, fill the measure of their creation, and experience the satisfaction and joy that comes from knowing their true purpose and divine identity. The insatiable appetite for continued improvement, self-discovery, and a sense of purpose drives the NGOs and impels them to stay their course and reach their goals. The ability to remain focused, committed to the goal at hand, and tap into inner strength amid setbacks, personal adversity, and trials is a defining feature of Noble and Great Ones.

Noble Rulership does not occur instantaneously. It cannot be given, nor can it be taken, without permission. It is established by the light of Christ within us. It is perpetuated by the whisperings of the spirit of God. It is developed by a lifetime of selfless and charitable acts. It is proven by obedience to the will of God. And it is ratified by the ability to fill the measure of our creation, regardless of what trials, adversities, or opposition may befall us. The journey toward Noble Rulership begins and ends with just three words. It starts with Faith, Purpose, and Possibilities, and it ends with Fear, Apathy, and Doubt (FAD).

Noble Rulership requires a mindset that is as different as good versus evil, light versus darkness, or right against wrong. It can be acknowledged by the first words we express as we awaken and begin our day. The mindset I am referring to is Optimism versus Pessimism.

Optimism emanates from the light of Christ we all have by virtue of our creator. Pessimism is just the opposite. Its origin emanates and is perpetuated by Lucifer himself, who seeks to make all men as miserable as he has chosen to become. His promptings are easily discerned. They are degrading and descending whisperings of pessimism and chatter of negativity that are customarily designed to weaken, wound, and displace our sense of divinity and purpose with a false sense of inadequacy, inability, and unworthiness.

We must always remember, "It's not about proportions, it's what's in the glass that matters most." You have a divine origin and purpose for being here at this place, at this time, and for God's purposes. A hallowed and optimistic encouragement emanates from Him that resonates deep within your soul and is always present. It has the power and ability you need to persevere and overcome any pain, suffering, and personal adversity you may be experiencing. The spirit of God burns deeply from within the soul and has the power to uplift, inspire, and motivate us all.

Wisdom, Stature, and Favor with God and Mankind

As Noble Rulers come to know themselves, control themselves, and give of themselves, they can discover and recognize their origins, their purposes, and their destinies. The obituary of their lives and the innumerable acts of service they rendered for humanity are a testament to their selflessness, service, and sacrifice. NGOs always place substance before quantity or image. They are ingrained to seek wisdom, stature, and favor with God and their fellow man. Their journey of continual self-improvement and determination to bless the lives of others is perpetual.

Noble and Great Ones are divinely chosen, foreordained, and purposely driven vessels. Their humanitarian acts reflect the divine gifts they possess and their accomplishments reach unprecedented heights and established new standards for other Noble and Great Ones to build on. One final word on the qualities and characteristics of NGOs. Their ability to let their lights shine so that others may see their good works and glorify God is boundless and commendable. In mastering their disciplines, their accomplishments often appear seemingly easy due to their special gifts and talents. The euphoria they experience from their accomplishments comes from knowing they are magnifying their gifts and talents and filling the measure of their creation.

Making It Look Easy

We will identify and introduce you to individuals who ruled or dominated their respective fields and disciplines in the chapters ahead. These individuals were selected for performance levels, achievements, and their moral influence on humanity.

Although their accomplishments were measurably great by definition, in some instances their nobility and contributions to humanity may have had room for improvement. I will let you be the judge of that.

These individuals are grouped into six categories: Emotion, Athletics, Spirituality, Intellect, Empathy, and Resiliency (EASIER). We will share a brief biography of those individuals who reflect one or more of the hallmark traits of an NGO, their domination and rulership within the six disciplines, and how they made their abilities look E.A.S.I.E.R. than other competitors.

These NGOs are people who lived extraordinary lives and exhibited great focus, determination, and purpose. Their perseverance and progression throughout their lives, through personal strife and adversity, emulated a path very few of us are willing to follow, let alone sustain. These individuals are the epitome of determination, inspiration, enlightenment, and improvement.

Equality Versus Difference

Equality and equal rights are noble aspirations that emanate from the heavens. The Holy Bible teaches that God is no respecter of persons. He loves all His children equally.

Whether you are male, female, or genderless; old, middle-aged, or young; bonded or free; black, white, or whatever color you choose. Whatever your present circumstance may be, it is His work and glory that you live a happy and purposeful life, that you check in often, and that you recognize His hand in your life and seek His guidance.

He has blessed each of us with an enlightened conscience, aka the Light of Christ, to help us choose the best course of action. We ought always to remember that doing what is right is paramount to asserting one's personal rights.

We can learn from history the mistakes made by those who assert their rights at the expense of doing what is right. One great example is the American Revolution, when the British monarchy exercised its perceived right of taxation while omitting the principle of representation. The great lesson in this instance is well reiterated and represented in the Book of Proverbs, which warns, "Pride goeth before destruction." (Proverbs 16:18)

Other Qualities Inherent in NGOs

NGOs, by nature, are laden with the noble qualities of Godliness. The traits within them include, but are not limited to, integrity, compassion, charity, diligence, authenticity, humility, faith, courage, optimism, virtue, spirituality, knowledge, intelligence, patience, obedience, temperance, persistence, endurance, and self-mastery. NGOs are recognized by the overabundance of one or more of these qualities.

In almost every instance, NGOs uncover and begin magnifying their gifts and talents early in life. This gives them a tremendous advantage in later life. As Ralph Waldo Emerson taught, "That which we persist in doing becomes easier to do, not that the nature of the thing has changed but that our power to do has increased."

Nobility and Greatness Is Within You

If your name does not exist in scripture, a history book, or Wikipedia, it does not mean you lack nobility or greatness.

Many individuals who lived extremely Noble lives preferred solidarity and privacy rather than seeking public acclaim or recognition. Others who accomplish acts of greatness relish the limelight and fame. Yet many of these individuals could do a great deal more acts of nobility through service efforts, sponsorships, charitable donations, and public outreach programs.

Some of them may look back on their lives with regret for having done less than they could have in helping others. Others may reminisce about the past, wondering how much further in life they might have gotten if only "such and such" had not happened. And some may acknowledge the ardent journey they made to reach the pinnacle of greatness in their vocation or discipline.

Connecting the Dots and Angels in Our Midst

In the following pages, you will read brief biographies of individuals who achieved tremendous accomplishments and whose lives and efforts left an imprint on their circles of influence, their countries, and in some instances, the course of history.

Many of these individuals risked life and limb, courageously pressing forward amidst seemingly insurmountable odds to accomplish their objectives. The sequential order of these individuals has nothing to do with the magnitude of their contributions or the degrees of nobility within them.

As you read the accomplishments of these individuals, take a moment to consider their greatness, worthiness, and impact of their results and those who were influenced by the outcome.

Once you have made your evaluation ask yourself this question, "Was the ratio between nobility and greatness equal, or did one outweigh the other? Next, ask yourself these three questions, how did it impact the individual? Did they treat the accomplishment as a destination or as a clearing from which all things are possible? Did the individual revel in their achievements, or did they fall to their knees and give thanks to their maker?

When reflecting on the individual successes of the individuals you read about, also reflect upon your own journey and the milestone events experienced in your life.

Noteworthy events and poignant experiences are rarely a matter of coincidence or good fortune. Rather, they are most often divine intervention with purposeful intent that shape our lives and allow us the opportunity of influencing others for good.

As you connect your dots, may you recognize your self-worth. There is untapped nobility and greatness within you yet to be acknowledged, extracted, and unleashed.

Defining moments will come to us all at some point in our lives. We have control over how we choose our responses. The choices range from a "Why Me? I Cannot Handle This! Cancel Me Now!! Tap-Out Experience" to an "Ah-Ha" moment that puts us on the path to greatness. The difference in which we choose results from our relationship with God and the advocacy, compassion, and service extended by others who seemingly appear out of nowhere when they are needed the most. Believe in God, expect the rescuer will come, and see the miracle. There are no coincidences in life, just miracles!

In Hebrews, chapter 13, the Apostle Paul declared, "Be not forgetful to entertain strangers for thereby some have entertained Angels unawares. Remember them that are in bonds, as bound with them; and them which suffer adversity, as being yourselves also in the body." (Hebrews 13:2-3)

May we all strive to be Angels for one another.

CHAPTER 4

The Emotional Rulers

Webster's online dictionary defines emotion as a conscious mental reaction (such as anger or fear) subjectively experienced as a strong feeling directed toward a specific outcome or object. Emotion impacts physiological and behavioral changes in the body. It has a significant impact on an individual's coping skills, physical and mental performance, and interactions with others.

Emotions impact our determination and resolve to overcome adversity and setbacks in life, garner added strength from within and from on high, and press forward overcoming every obstacle set before us to fill the measure of our creation and have joy. Our emotions impact whether a defining moment or circumstance will evoke fight or flight, compassion or contempt, faith or fear, condemnation, or forgiveness. Emotion is the greatest determinant in whether we rise to the occasion or wallow in grief or self-pity. It determines our attitude and altitude and is the difference between rational and irrational thought, hope and despair, success and failure. Simply put, our emotions can make or break us and impact our eternal destiny.

According to author Jane Austen in her book *Mansfield Park*, emotion is both resolute and fragile. Some events may appear branded in vivid details to the hard drive within our brains, while other events may be completely erased just seconds after the occurrence. Evidence from memory experts suggests the mind is more apt to remember bad experiences rather than good experiences.

One such expert, Elizabeth Kensinger, suggests, "When people recall significant, emotional events in their lives, such as their wedding day or the birth of their first child, they're generally greatly confident about how well they remember the details of the event."

But whether or not this confidence is warranted is debatable because details remembered with confidence often are not exactly correct, according to a review of research on emotional memories. Memories are generally prone to distortion over time.

However, researchers have found some evidence to suggest that emotional memories are more resistant to the decay processes that wear away at all memories with time. While we might not remember complete details about a bad event we experience, the details remembered about a negative event are more likely to be accurate.

"It's clear that there's something very kind of special and prioritized about how we remember those emotional experiences," said Kessinger, whose review was published in the August 2007 issue of the journal *Current Directions in Psychological Science*.

Emotional Performance

According to Dr. Shahram Heshmat, Ph.D., in an article on Psychologytoday.com, "A normal function of emotion is to enhance memory in order to improve recall of experiences that have importance or relevance for our survival. Emotion acts like a highlighter pen that emphasizes certain aspects of experiences to make them more memorable. Memory formation involves registering information (encoding), processing, storage, and retrieval."

According to Dr. Heshmat, emotion affects all the phases of memory formation. Here is how:

1. Attention: Attention guides our focus to select what is most relevant for our lives and is normally associated with novelty. Nothing focuses the mind like a surprise. For example, although one may thoroughly enjoy a particular conversation, the same conversation a second time around would be dull. Emotional intensity acts to narrow the scope of attention so that a few objects are emphasized at the expense of many others. Focusing upon a very narrow area allows for optimal use of our limited attentional capacity.

2. Consolidation of a memory: Most of the information we acquire is forgotten and never makes it into long-term memory. When we learn a complex problem, the short-term memory is freed up and the action becomes automatic. Emotionally charged events are remembered better than those of neutral events. You will never forget some events, such as the joy of the birth of your first child or the horror of the 9/11 terrorist attack. The stress hormones, epinephrine and cortisol, enhance memory and consolidate memory contents. In evolutionary terms, it is logical for us to imprint dangerous situations with extra clarity so that we may avoid them in the future.

3. Memory recall: Memories of painful emotional experiences linger far longer than those involving physical pain. There is an old saying that "sticks and stones can break your bones, but words can never hurt you." On the contrary, evidence shows that hurt feelings could be worse than physical pain. In the words of Maya Angelou, "I've learned that people will forget what you said, people will forget what you did, but people will never forget how you made them feel."

4. Priming: Memories are often triggered or primed by one's environment. Priming refers to activating behavior through the power of unconscious suggestion. Researchers have found that people who were made to think of self-discipline (by having to unscramble sentences about it) immediately made more future-oriented snack choices than those given sentences about self-indulgence. In this case, the goal stored in long-term memory is retrieved and placed in short-term (or working) memory. Similarly, the concept of a library causes people to speak more softly.

5. Mood memory: Our current emotional state facilitates the recall of experiences that had a similar emotional tone. When we are in a happy mood, we tend to recall pleasant events and vice versa. This is because moods bring different associations to mind. For example, recalling positive childhood experiences while in a good mood. Being in a bad mood primes a person to think about negative things.

6. Blanking out: Stress can lead to memory

deficit, such as the common experience of mentally blanking during a high-pressure examination or interview. Thus, worrying about how you will perform on a test may actually contribute to a lower test score. In general, anxiety influences cognitive performance in a curvilinear manner (an inverted U-curve). This phenomenon is known as the Yerkes–Dodson Law. When arousal levels are too low (boredom) or too high (anxiety or fear), performance is likely to suffer. Under situations of low arousal, the mind is unfocused. In contrast, under high stimulation situations, the focus of attention is too narrow, and important information may be lost. The optimal situation is moderate arousal.

7. Duration neglect (Peak-End rule): The way we remember events is not necessarily a recollection of every particular moment. Instead, we tend to remember and overemphasize the peak (best or worst) moment and the last moment, and neglect the duration of an experience. This explains why a bad ending ruins the whole experience. For example, when you remember your summer vacation to Canada, there is just too much information to evaluate whether it was an enjoyable trip. So, you apply the peak-end rule and more heavily weight the best moment and the most recent moment. In summary, the "Wow Effect" is what gets our attention, while also narrowing our focus.

Most of our life experiences rarely make it past short-term memory. Those that do are generally emotionally charged, life-threatening, and adrenaline pumping experiences.

Emotional pain lingers far longer than physical pain. Environment can influence behavior by tapping into our unconscious thoughts of self-indulgence or self-discipline. Our current emotional state can evoke past emotional tones. Hence positive childhood events can evoke a good mood.

Anxiety and stress hinder personal performance and progression and can cause blank-out or memory loss. Low arousal causes boredom, while high arousal causes anxiety, fear, and stress. Moderate arousal is optimal. Duration neglect means our mind tends to remember the best, worst, and last moments more than any other moments of an experience.

What is Emotional Intelligence?

According to Drs. Travis Bradberry and Jean Greaves, high Emotional Intelligence (EQ) trumps high IQ when it comes to personal achievement and performance. Emotional intelligence amounts to 58% of your job performance. 90% of top performers rank highly in EQ and individuals with high EQs earn, on average, $29,000 more annually than their lower EQ counterparts.

So, what exactly is emotional intelligence? Here's what Drs. Bradberry and Greaves say on the subject, "Emotional intelligence is the 'something' in each of us that is a bit intangible. It affects how we manage behavior, navigate social complexities, and make personal decisions that achieve positive results."

In essence, emotional intelligence is your ability to recognize and understand emotions in yourself and others, and your ability to use this awareness to manage your behavior and relationships.

The four core skills that make up an individual's EQ are paired under two primary competencies: personal competence and social competence.

Personal competence is a combination of self-awareness and self-management skills, focusing more on you individually than on your interactions with other people. Personal competence is your ability to stay aware of your emotions and manage your behavior and tendencies.

Self-Awareness is your ability to accurately perceive your emotions and stay aware of them as they happen. Self-Management is your ability to use awareness of your emotions to stay flexible and positively direct your behavior.

Social competence comprises social awareness and relationship management skills. The bearer has the ability to understand other people's moods, behaviors, and motives to improve the quality of their relationships.

Social-Awareness is the ability to accurately pick up on emotions in other people and understand what is really going on. Relationship Management is the ability to use awareness of one's own emotions and the emotions of others to manage interactions successfully.

Intelligence is your ability to learn, and it is equally the same at age 15 as it is at age 50. On the other hand, emotional intelligence is a flexible set of skills that can be acquired, practiced, and enhanced.

Although some people are naturally more emotionally intelligent than others, you can develop high emotional intelligence even if you are not born with a high degree of it.

The communication between the emotional and rational areas of the brain is the physical source of emotional intelligence. The pathway for emotional intelligence starts in the brain, at the spinal cord. Your primary senses enter here and must travel to the front of your brain before you can think rationally about your experience.

However, first they travel through the limbic system, the place where emotions are generated. Because of this, we often have an emotional reaction to events before our rational mind engages. Emotional intelligence requires effective communication between the rational and emotional centers of the brain.

Plasticity is the term neurologists use to describe the brain's ability to change. Your brain grows new connections as you learn new skills. The change is gradual, as your brain cells develop new connections to speed the efficiency of new skills acquired.

Using strategies to increase your emotional intelligence allows the billions of microscopic neurons lining the road between your brain's rational and emotional centers to branch off small "arms" (much like a tree) to reach out to the other cells. A single cell can grow 15,000 connections with its neighbors.

This chain reaction of growth ensures it is easier to kick a new behavior into action in the future. Once you train your brain by repeatedly using new emotional intelligence strategies, emotionally intelligent behaviors become habits.

EQ has an impact on nearly every aspect of our lives. It affects our choices and decisions, our relationships with others, and the difference between optimism and pessimism, compassion and contempt, wisdom and bewilderment, peace and chaos. More than IQ, EQ can determine your career success, longevity, and assertion in the business marketplace.

High EQ Characteristics

Mark Murphy, author of the New York Times Best Seller *Hiring for Attitude*, believes five workplace indicators serve as a litmus test to determine individuals with or without high emotional intelligence. Here are the qualities he shared in a Forbes interview article on *5 Signs of High Emotional Intelligence*:

> Sign No.1 – They handle criticism well, without denial, blame, excuses, or anxiety. In other words, they weigh, ponder, and consider criticism constructively and without retribution.
>
> Sign No. 2 – They remain open-minded and non-judgmental. They have a knack for helping people get things right.
>
> Sign No. 3 – They are good listeners. They have learned to block out the emotions of the communicator and hear what the person is saying.
>
> Sign No. 4 – They do not sugarcoat the truth. They understand that tough messages need to be shared and heard.
>
> Sign No. 5 – They apologize when they are wrong rather than prove why they are right. They recognize and admit when they are wrong.

Now that we have a foundation to understand better how our brains function, let us identify the qualities in those who excel in their ability to control their emotions and improve their performance.

Emotional Rulers Set Attainable Goals and Boundaries

In the article *10 Qualities of People With High Emotional Intelligence* from *Inc.* magazine, these are the primary determinants that reveal your EQ ranking:

- They're not perfectionists. Perfectionists wait for every last shred of evidence, resulting in a slow start and slower results. Individuals with high EQ recognize perfection is an illusion and that procrastination can be a deal-breaker. Individuals with high EQ recognize the opportunity cost of waiting too long to complete a task or project. They know how to balance work and play.

- They distinguish between when it is time to work and when it is time to play. They plan when it comes to work and play and get the most from every moment in each.

- They are not workaholics; rather, they recognize the value and essential benefits from both activities.

- They make time for their physical, emotional, mental, and spiritual well-being.

- They embrace change. People with high EQ treat change as a necessity of life. Fear of change is a major deterrent in people's lives; it can stifle career advancement and hamper relationships. When faced with an unexpected situation or circumstance, individuals who possess high EQ either have a prepared strategy in advance or simply adjust and improvise.

- They do not get easily distracted. People with high EQ have focus and can remain on task without being easily distracted. They prioritize well, execute quickly, and accomplish the task at hand effectively, efficiently, and ahead of schedule.

- They're empathetic. Individuals who possess high EQ relate well to others, show compassion to others, and help others in need. They are curious to learn from others and ask intelligent questions when meeting new acquaintances to get to know them.

- They know their strengths and weaknesses.

- Emotionally intelligent people are effective at delegation. They live the credo immortalized by Clint Eastwood in the movie *Magnum Force*, "A man's got to know his limitations." Not only are they good delegators, but they also have the added ability to leverage their gifts and talents by aligning themselves with the right people to ensure success.

- They're self-motivated. If some watch things happen, some make things happen, and some wonder what happened, individuals possessing high EQ are most certainly those from the middle group. They are ambitiously hard-working and goal-oriented people. Being a real go-getter, even at a young age, is another quality possessed by people with EQ. They do not dwell in the past.

Here are three more traits of EQ nobility:

- People with high EQ forgive quickly. They mend easily and restore relationships unconditionally. In their minds, there is no tomorrow; there is only today. They are driven each day by purpose, goals, and objectives. The past is history, the future a mystery, and today is a gift. That is why it is called the present.

- They focus on the positive. Emotionally intelligent people are good at crossword puzzles and great at problem solving. Rather than dwelling on the negative, they focus on what is positive. They fully understand and acknowledge decisions and consequences they have control over and those beyond their control. They are optimistic and choose to spend their time with other positive people, rather than cynics or complainers.

- They set boundaries. Individuals with high EQ may appear to be pushovers because of their empathy and desire to help others, but that would be a misjudgment. They have established boundaries and know how to diplomatically and graciously disagree or say no when necessary. This helps these individuals maintain peace, balance, and consistency. It also shields them from becoming overwhelmed, burned out, and stressed due to their many commitments and directions they have taken.

Top EQ Rulers Who Caught My Attention

Audrey Hepburn was one of the greatest actresses in Hollywood. Following World War II, she chose to become a Hollywood actress and caught the attention of William Wyler, director of the movie *Roman Holiday*. Wyler described her as, "One that had everything I was looking for: charm, innocence, and talent. She also had a great sense of humor. She was absolutely enchanting!"

Wyler gave her the main role in *Roman Holiday*, ahead of Elizabeth Taylor, and the rest is history. As a humanitarian, Hepburn was active as the Goodwill Ambassador of UNICEF. She considered herself one of the lucky ones and dedicated her later years to helping children in poverty-stricken parts around the world.

Oprah Winfrey is one of the most influential women in history. A talk-show host, actress, producer, and philanthropist, she rose above the degrading conditions of her early life — being abandoned by her mother, sexually abused by members of her family, and losing a child as an unwed teenager. While any one of these horrific experiences could have become a crutch and justification for failure, Winfrey used them to strengthen her resolve and forge her determination for success. She took strength from her grandmother, claiming she instilled a positive sense about herself.

Her TV success is based on timely, good-oriented intuition about what an audience wants: less-tabloid formats, broader topics, and sharp turnaround on various social issues. Her talent for making people open up about the most intimate things has become so famous that the entire phenomenon deserved its own name: The Rarefication, just like the power of her opinion: The Oprah effect.

What role does EQ play when it comes to adversity? Is there a corollary between the two? High IQ does not always trump high EQ. One example of this is Apple co-founder Steve Jobs, who earned a 32 on the ACT at a time when a 24 is now equivalent to a 28. According to Mensa, a 29 at that time is still a qualifying score for membership. So, we can assume that it is in the neighborhood of the 98th percentile. To earn a 32 would likely be in the neighborhood of a 35 today and would equate to the 99.6th percentile.

Despite his high IQ, Jobs would suddenly "flip," taking an idea that he had mocked (maybe your idea) and embracing it passionately — and as his own — without ever acknowledging that his view had changed. "He has this ability to change his mind and completely forget his old opinion about something," says a former close colleague who asked not to be named. "It's weird. He can say, 'I love white; white is the best.' And then three months later say, 'Black is the best; white is not the best.' He does not live with his mistake. It evaporates." Jobs would rationalize it all by simply explaining, "We're doing what's right today."

Jobs was a global cultural guru, shaping what entertainment we watch, how we listen to music, and the objects we use to work and play. He changed the game for entire industries.

Jobs was also among the most controversial figures in business. He oozed smug superiority and laced his public comments with ridicule of Apple's rivals, which he cast as mediocre, evil, and — worst of all — lacking taste. No CEO was more willful, or more brazen, at making his own rules, in ways both good and bad. And no CEO was more personally identified with — and controlling — the day-to-day affairs of his business.

Interestingly, Jobs viewed himself less as a mogul than as an artist. He considered himself Apple's creator-in-chief and listed himself as "co-inventor" on 103 separate Apple patents, on everything from the iPod's user interface to the support system for the glass staircase used in Apple's dazzling retail stores.

Jobs' social and interpersonal abuses are also legendary. He often parked his Mercedes in handicapped spaces. He was known to periodically reduce subordinates to tears. And he would fire employees in angry tantrums.

Yet many of his top deputies at Apple worked with him for years. Even some of those who departed during his reign said that although it was often brutal working for Jobs, and that Jobs tended to hog all the credit, they have never done better work.

History, of course, is littered with tales of combustible geniuses. What is astounding is how well Jobs performed atop a large public company, by its nature a collaborative enterprise.

"The degree to which people in Silicon Valley are afraid of Jobs is unbelievable. He made people feel terrible; he made people cry. But he was almost always right, and even when he was wrong, it was so creative it was still amazing," stated Palo Alto venture capitalist Jean-Louis Gasse, a former Apple executive who once worked with Jobs: "Democracies do not make great products. You need a competent tyrant."

How Jobs pulled all this off — how this bundle of conflicting behaviors coexisted, to spectacular effect, in a single human being — remains a puzzle, even though more than a dozen books have been written about him.

CHAPTER 5

The Athletic Rulers

I n the late 1970s, ABC's *Wide World of Sports* coined a phrase that has been indelibly emblazoned in the minds of traditionalists and baby boomers since it was first introduced. "The thrill of victory and the agony of defeat" showcased the physical, mental, emotional, and spiritual strength of athletes driven to overcome obstacles of all kinds, including financial, psychological, and physical barriers, to earn a spot on arguably the single greatest stage for athletic achievement, recognition, fame, and fortune on planet earth...the Olympics.

The original Olympic Games were dedicated to the Olympian Gods and were held, as you might suspect, in Olympia, Greece, in 776 BC. The games continued for 1200 years, with the final games ending in 393 AD. Following a 1503-year hiatus, the games returned to Greece in 1896 with the venue changed to Athens.

Today, the Olympics draws five billion viewers from every nationality, country, and niche on earth. Athletes that reach the pinnacle of their performance today, if recent history holds true, and it usually does, will enjoy a global platform that can elevate a champion to fame and fortune almost instantly.

The quest to break a world record in the Olympics requires a superior attitude, amplitude, and aptitude to benefit the athlete. The level of talent, commitment, and self-awareness of the athlete's potential for greatness must be internalized within the athlete to accomplish their goal and be successful.

Endurance, athleticism, spirituality, intelligence, emotion, and resilience are all active ingredients found in Olympic Champions. The athlete's journey toward self-realization, the ability to look beyond perceived shortcomings, overcome adversity, and fill the unique measure of one's creation is the elixir that fuels athletes, draws viewership, and inspires self-discovery, perpetuates hope, and drives loyalty and patriotism.

Although we may applaud the athletic achievement, it is the passion, purpose, character, commitment, and relentless drive of their noble quest that we remember most. Constant improvement toward a worthy goal and lifting others to higher ground is both noble and great. These attributes have been heralded throughout all generations. They are revered throughout history and are taught in our schools, churches, mosques, and synagogues.

Let us set the table now by identifying the top 50 sports, their approximate viewing audience, the ruling athletes represented in these various sports, and their impact on society relative to the lifestyle they lived. You may be surprised at the results. Sports in some countries have a larger impact and influence due to population size. Therefore, they naturally have a larger viewing audience. Sports that may be relatively small or obscure in your own country may be hugely popular in the country of its origin.

For example, table tennis and cricket may not be hugely popular in the United States. However, watch a table tennis match in Asia or a cricket match in India or Australia and your opinion of the sport may change quickly. In addition, emerging sports with accelerated popularity may wane in viewership and seemingly disappear almost overnight, such as Major League Baseball when 500 players traded their team uniforms for military duty during World War II.

The sports selected represent the highest participatory rankings listed in the order of the greatest opportunity to impact individuals and influence and increase participation in that sport. These sports possess the greatest opportunity to showcase and immortalize some of the most gifted athletes the world has ever known.

The Top 50 sports listed per viewing audience are:

1. Olympics – 5B
2. Soccer – 3.2B
3. Cricket – 2.2B
4. Field Hockey – 2B
5. Tennis – 1B
6. Volleyball – 900M
7. Table Tennis — 850M
8. Baseball – 500M
9. Golf – 450M
10. Motocross – 450M
11. Basketball – 400M
12. American football – 400M
13. Boxing – 320M
14. Badminton – 316M
15. Running – 243M

16. Motor Sports – 177M

17. Cycling – 170M

18. Triathlon – 111M

19. Drag Racing – 111M

20. Canoeing – 82M

21. Trampolining – 50M

22. Extreme sports/Games – 37M

23. Freestyle skiing – 30M

24. Snowboarding – 25.5M

25. Bobsleigh/Luge – 22M

26. Snooker – 18M

27. Water Sports – 18M

28. Mixed Martial Arts – 17M

29. Rugby Union – 16M

30. Moto/GP – 15M

31. NASCAR – 14M

32. Water Polo — 9.9M

33. Horse Racing – 9M

34. Gymnastics – 8M

35. Rowing – 7.6M

36. Handball – 6.5M

37. Figure Skating – 6.5M

38. Cross Country Skiing — 6.2M

39. Wrestling — 6M

40. Downhill Skiing – 6M

41. Diving – 5.8M

42. Speed Skating – 5.6M

43. Rally – 4.8M

44. Rugby League – 4.5M

45. Indy car – 4.1M

46. Shooting – 3.7M

47. Touring Cars – 3.7M

48. Weightlifting – 3.6M

49. Windsurfing – 3.5M

50. Judo – 3.2M

The Ruling Class of Athletes

The following athletes were chosen by virtue of their athleticism and accomplishments in their respective fields. They represent the top 15 sports in terms of popularity and audience viewership.

#1 The Olympics — Michael Phelps and Nadia Comăneci were two of the greatest Olympians of all time. Phelps was born in Baltimore, Maryland, and raised in Towson, Maryland. The youngest of three children, Phelps, (nicknamed the "Baltimore Bullet," the "Flying Fish," and, on occasion, "Gomer," for his larger than average ears), began swimming at the age of seven, due in part to the influence of his sisters and to provide him with an outlet for his boundless energy.

While in the sixth grade, Phelps was diagnosed with attention deficit hyperactivity disorder (ADHD). He achieved his first national record at age 12 and began to train with Bob Bowman at the North Baltimore Aquatic Club. Three years later, Phelps qualified for the 2000 Summer Olympics, the youngest male to make a U.S.

Olympic swim team in 68 years. While he did not win an Olympic medal, he did make the finals and finished fifth in the 200-meter butterfly. That same year, Phelps became the youngest male ever to set a world record while swimming in the World Championship Trials.

By winning eight gold medals at the 2008 Beijing Games, Phelps surpassed the previous record of seven gold medals set by fellow swimmer Mark Spitz. Phelps holds an unprecedented 23 gold medals and 28 total medals in his Olympic career. His lifetime medal count is an astounding 83 medals in major international long-course competition with 66 gold, 14 silvers, and three bronze medals. Phelps's record-breaking performances earned him the World Swimmer of the Year Award seven times, American Swimmer nine times, and the FINA Swimmer of the Year Award in 2012. His Olympic success in 2008 earned him the Sports Illustrated magazine's Sportsman of the Year award.

Following those Summer Olympics, Phelps established the Michael Phelps Foundation, which focuses on swimming and promoting healthier lifestyles. His coach Bob Bowman described Phelps as "a solitary man with a rigid focus prior to racing and incredibly invested in the success of the people he cares about. He's unbelievably kind-hearted."

Nadia Elena Comăneci was born in Onești, Romania. Her mother named her Nadia after the heroine in a Russian film named Nadya, the diminutive version of the Russian name Nadezhda, which means "hope."

Comăneci began gymnastics in kindergarten with a local team called Flacăra ("The Flame"). At age six, she was chosen to attend Béla Károlyi's experimental gymnastics school when Károlyi spotted her and a friend turning cartwheels in a schoolyard during recess. Károlyi was looking for gymnasts he could train at an early age. When recess ended, the girls ran inside the building and Károlyi went from one classroom to the next trying to find them. He picked Comăneci, while her friend Viorica Dumitru went on to be one of Romania's top ballerinas.

In 1969, at her first Romanian National Championships competition and only eight years old, she finished in 13th place. Following the competition, Károlyi gave her a doll to remind her never to place 13th again. She never did. A year later, she became the youngest gymnast ever to win the Romanian Nationals. In 1971, during her first international competition, she won her first all-around title and contributed significantly to the team Gold Medal.

Comăneci became a star at the 1976 Summer Olympics held in Montreal, Canada. At just 14 years, her routine on the uneven bars earned a perfect ten. It was the first ten awarded in modern Olympic gymnastics history. At the time, Omega SA, the traditional Olympics scoreboard manufacturer, asked if four digits would be necessary for gymnastics and was told that a perfect score of 10.00 was impossible. Nadia's perfect score was thus displayed as 1.00 rather than 10.00.

During that Olympics, Comăneci would earn six more perfect scores en route to capturing the all-around, beam, and bars titles, with one bronze medal for the floor exercise.

Comăneci became the first Romanian gymnast to win the Olympic all-around title and still holds the record as the youngest Olympic gymnastics all-around champion ever. Her record is unbeatable now that the Olympic Committee has raised the minimum requirement to 16 years of age.

Comăneci has been active in many charities and international organizations. In 1999, she became the first athlete invited to speak at the United Nations, launching the 2000 International Year of Volunteers. She is on the International Board of Directors for the Special Olympics and is vice president of the Muscular Dystrophy Association Board of Directors. She personally funded the construction and operation of the Nadia Comăneci Children's Clinic in Bucharest, which provides low-cost and free medical and social support to Romanian children.

In 2003, the Romanian government appointed her as an honorary consul general of Romania to the United States. In 1984 and 2004, she received the Olympic Order, the highest award of the International Olympic Committee. She is the only person to have received this honor twice and is also its youngest recipient. She is an inductee of the International Gymnastics Hall of Fame.

#2 Soccer — Edson Arantes do Nascimento, or "Pelé" (Pronounced Pay-Lay) as referred to by most soccer fans. Recognized by the International Athletic Committee as the "Athlete of the Century," most football (or soccer fans if you live in the U.S.) consider Pelé as the greatest football player of all time. Playing for Brazil, Pelé was a prolific striker and the only player in history who won the World Cup three times.

Pelé was fast, agile, creative, intelligent, technically skilled, and precise in his footwork and passing. As a gifted athlete, he had a remarkable sense of goal and timing.

Pelé was beyond being an achiever; he was a pioneer and innovator and is often cited and remembered for his patented "Bicycle Kick." From his start at age 16 until his retirement 22 years later, he was THE football icon, eclipsing all other contenders.

Pelé's career records are almost unimaginable. He still holds the world record for most goals scored. In six of his matches, he scored five goals, in 30 matches he scored four goals, and in 92 of his matches he scored three goals. Perhaps his most exciting and memorable score came in Maracanã Stadium in Rio De Janeiro when, on a penalty kick, he scored his 1000th goal. The crowd let out a deafening roar and even the opposing fans celebrated.

In the 22 years that Pelé dominated soccer, he did more for "goodwill and friendship than all the ambassadors ever appointed," stated J. B. Pinheiro, the Brazilian Ambassador to the United Nations, at Pelé's retirement. Following his career, Pelé continued to stay active in humanitarian activities, including an ambassador of goodwill for UNICEF and an ambassador of football around the world. He lived a noble life, and his greatness was both lifting for the sport of soccer and inspirational to those athletes that would follow.

#3 Cricket — Donald Bradman began playing cricket in his youth when he devised his own solo cricket game, using a cricket stump as a bat, a golf ball, and a water tank, mounted on a curved brick stand as a paved area behind his home. The golf ball rebounded at high speed and unpredictable angles, helping him develop timing and reactions to high-speed pitching. He hit his first century at age 12.

In his professional life, he was referred to as "The Don." Widely recognized as the greatest Test Batsman of all time, he maintained a career test batting average of 99.94, a statistic often cited as the greatest achievement by any sportsman in any major sport. Bradman became Australia's sporting idol at the height of the Great Depression. In 2001, more than 50 years after Bradman's retirement as a Test player, Prime Minister John Howard of Australia called him the "greatest living Australian."

In December 1985, Bradman was the first of 120 inaugural inductees into the Sport Australia Hall of Fame. He spoke of his philosophy for considering the stature of athletes, "When considering the stature of an athlete or for that matter any person, I set great stock in certain qualities which I believe to be essential in addition to skill. They are that the person conducts his or her life with dignity, integrity, courage, and perhaps most of all, with modesty. These virtues are completely compatible with pride, ambition, and competitiveness." By his philosophy, the life he lived, and the inspiration he was to others, Bradman lived a noble and great life.

#4 Field Hockey — Jamie Dwyer and Luciana Aymar are the two best field hockey players to have ever played the sport.

Born in 1979 in Australia, Dwyer lifted his first hockey stick at age four. He was named the world's best field hockey player in 2004, 2007, 2009, 2010, and 2011.

Dwyer played many sports throughout childhood, excelling in both cricket and hockey. At age 15, he had the choice of accepting a cricket scholarship that would mean he would need to move to Brisbane. He declined the offer because of his ardent desire to one day compete at the Olympics.

His dream was to win an Olympic Gold Medal and represent Australia. He fulfilled his childhood when he broke a 48-year Australian Gold Medal drought by scoring the winning goal in the Gold medal match in the 2004 Summer Olympics. It was the Kookaburra's first Olympic Gold medal.

Luciana Aymar was born in Rosario, Argentina, in 1977. She is the only player in history to receive the FIH Player of the Year Award eight times. She is without argument the best female hockey player in history. Her interest in field hockey began when she was seven years of age. She was 16 years old when she made her playing debut for the Argentina senior team, becoming the youngest player in the team's history.

Aymar is known for her fast pace and dribbling skills. She is often compared to the Argentinian footballer Diego Maradona, bearing his nickname of "La Maga" (The Magician) and "The Maradona of Field Hockey."

In 2008, the International Hockey Federation named Aymar a Legend of Hockey. She had the honor of carrying the flag for Argentina at the opening ceremony of the 2007 Pan American Games held in Rio de Janeiro, Brazil, which she repeated at the 2012 Summer Olympic Games, held in London, England.

#5 Tennis — Roger Federer was born in 1981. The career accomplishments of Federer are nothing less than astounding. He maintained the world's number one position for 237 weeks. He reached 27 men's Grand Slam singles championship matches and won 17 of them, including 10 in a row starting with Wimbledon in 2005 and ending with the 2007 U.S. Open. Federer shares two Open Era records, one with Pete Sampras for most Wimbledon wins (7) and one with Jimmy Connors and Pete Sampras for most U.S. Open wins (5). Federer and Rafael Nadal became one of the greatest rivalries in men's tennis history.

From a humanitarian viewpoint, Federer has been an active participant. In 2003, he established the Roger Federer Foundation to support disadvantaged children and provide them access to education and sports. He began supporting the South Africa-Swiss charity IMBEWU in 2004. IMBEWU helps children develop an interest in sports and social and health awareness.

Federer has auctioned Championship Tournament rackets to aid hurricane victims and arranged exhibitions assembling other tennis professionals for relief rallies, with proceeds given to tsunami victims. He has also raised money for earthquake victims.

He has been named a "Goodwill Ambassador" by UNICEF. His Nadal vs. Federer "Match for Africa" in 2010, held in Zurich and Madrid, raised over $4 million for the RafaNadal Foundation. In September 2011, in a South African poll, Federer was voted the second most trusted and respected person in the world, next to Nelson Mandela.

#6 Volleyball — Charles "Karch" Kiraly was born in 1960 and grew up in Santa Barbara, California. Karch began playing volleyball when he was only six years of age. His father, Dr. Laszlo Kiraly, a former member of the Hungarian Junior National team, was his greatest advocate and encourager to enter the sport. At 11 years of age, Kiraly, with his father at his side (literally), entered his first beach volleyball tournament.

In 1978, Kiraly enrolled at UCLA, majoring in biochemistry. Beginning his freshman year, he played outside hitter and setter on the Bruins' volleyball team opposite junior Sinjin Smith in the Bruins' 6-2 offense. In his freshman year, Kiraly led UCLA to the NCAA Men's Volleyball Championship. In his sophomore season, Karch led the Bruins to the finals again, where they lost to USC. UCLA reclaimed the top spot in Kiraly's junior season. Kiraly completed his college career with another title during his senior year.

During the four years that Kiraly played at UCLA, the Bruins compiled a 123-5 match record, with titles in 1979, 1981, and 1982. UCLA went undefeated in the 1979 and 1982 seasons. Kiraly received All-American honors all four years, and he was named the NCAA Volleyball Tournament Most Outstanding Player in 1981 and 1982. Kiraly graduated cum laude in June 1983, with a 3.34 cumulative GPA while earning a Bachelor of Science degree in Biochemistry. In 1992, Kiraly was inducted into the UCLA Hall of Fame and had his jersey retired.

Kiraly is the best all-around player the sport has ever seen. He led the U.S National Team to the gold medal in 1984 at the Summer Olympics. His team lost in pool play to Brazil and defeated them in the finals, making Kiraly the youngest player on the gold medal team. In the 1988 Summer Olympics, the team won its second gold medal, defeating the USSR. Kiraly was chosen as captain for the 1988 team in Seoul, Korea. FIVB named Kiraly the top player in the world in 1986 and 1988.

Kiraly is the 'winningest' player in the history of professional beach circuit volleyball. Kiraly won more than $3 million in prize money during his beach volleyball career and earned much more in endorsements. Kiraly won 148 professional beach volleyball titles and his beach record speaks for itself. In 24 of the 28 seasons he played beach volleyball, he claimed titles with 13 different playing partners.

#7 Table Tennis — Ma Long was born in 1988 in Anshan, Liaoning, China. Long has won a record five ITTF World Tour tournaments in a row, including a streak of 35 set wins. Ma is the best two-winged looper in table tennis history. His serves are visually deceptive, and his range of attacks are innumerable. He uses his backhand to block incoming loops. His opponents are surprised when he suddenly loops with his backhand, which he can do near or away from the table. He is a consistent chop blocker and uses this stroke to counter slow loops having heavy sidespin.

In 2006, at the Bremen World Team Championship, Long became the youngest world champion in history at just 18 years of age. Ma learned his fundamental play from Wang Hao and former Chinese National Team Coach Ma Kai Xuan. Before he reached 22 years of age, he had reached the finals of 11 ITTF World Tour tournaments and won eight of them. He won the Asian Cup and the World Tour Grand Finals twice and has made it to the Asian Championships final twice, winning in 2009.

#8 Baseball — Babe Ruth was the most gifted athlete in the history of baseball. In the *Sporting News* book *Baseball's 100 Greatest Players*, George Herman "Babe" Ruth is at the top of the list as the greatest baseball player to ever played the game. The Society for American Baseball Research went one step further, touting Ruth as the sport's greatest player.

What made Babe the best? Statistics. Ruth impacted baseball statistics like no other athlete ever has and maybe ever will. His overall statistics are staggering; he had a .342 career batting average, 2873 hits, 2217 RBIs, and, of course, 714 home runs.

As Leigh Montville points out in his biography of Ruth, *The Big Bam: The Life and Times of Babe Ruth*, these astonishing stats were accumulated during baseball's "dead-ball" era, during which games were played in huge, cavernous stadiums that made home runs and other big hits difficult to achieve.

His career home run record lasted nearly 40 years, until another legend, Hank Aaron, surpassed it. Ruth was part of seven World Series-winning teams, including the first four championships the New York Yankees ever won. Off the field, he is considered by many as the first true sports celebrity. Fans flocked to the ballparks to see him, and his hard-partying ways made him a legend to millions of people.

Ruth's prodigious power output changed the way the game was played. In 1920, his first season with the Yankees, Ruth hit 54 home runs, more than any team except the Philadelphia Phillies hit that season. He was the first player to hit 60 homers in a season, which he did in 1927. Any which way you assess his statistics, his achievements were remarkable.

The one blemish in his impeccable statistical qualities was his fondness for alcohol and self-indulgence. Considering his many accomplishments on the field, he missed the opportunity to become one of the greatest humanitarians in all of sports.

#9 Golf — Jack Nicholas was the greatest golfer ever, based on major championships. Nicholas won 18 Majors, two U.S. Amateur titles, and 73 PGA Tour wins. During his 25-year career, he won the Master's six times and all four majors in a row (three times). He finished in second place 19 times and third place nine times.

Nicklaus was born in Columbus, Ohio, and grew up in Upper Arlington, Ohio. He attended high school in Arlington, whose school mascot was called the Golden Bear, a nickname Nicklaus would soon be known by. Like his father, Nicholas was an all-around athlete during high school, competing successfully in football, baseball, tennis, and track and field.

Nicklaus began golfing at age 10. By 12 years of age, Nicklaus had won the first of five straight Ohio State Junior titles. At 13 years of age, he faced a mild bout with polio, broke 70, and became that year's youngest qualifier into the U.S. Junior Amateur. Before his 14th birthday, his handicap was +3.

In 1961, Nicklaus became the first player to win the individual title at the NCAA Championship and the U.S. Amateur in the same year. Nicklaus won the NCAA Big Ten Conference Championship that same year, maintaining a 72-hole aggregate of 283.

One year later, he won the U.S. Open, his first professional win, an event that sparked a rivalry between him and Arnold Palmer that would last for years to come. In 1966, he won the Master's Tournament the second year in a row. Later that year, he won The Open Championship, completing his first career slam of major championships.

Between 1971 and 1980, he won nine more majors to overtake Bobby Jones' record of 13 majors. In 1986, he became the oldest player ever to win the Masters at age 49. For the record, Nicklaus played in 23 official worldwide events in 1971, won eight, had 17 top-5 finishes, 20 top-10 finishes, and compiled a 5–1–0 record in that year's Ryder Cup competition. He joined the Senior's Tour in 1990, and over the next six years won ten more major championships.

In addition to playing golf, his off-the-course activities include golf course design, charity events, and book writing. To help perpetuate the game of golf globally, Nicklaus has designed golf courses in Asia, Australia, Canada, Europe, and Mexico.

As a humanitarian, Nicklaus and his wife Barbara serve as honorary chairman and chairwoman of the Nicklaus Children's Health Care Foundation, which provides valuable programs and services to more than 4,000 hospitalized children and their families, free of charge.

They also established "The Jake," a pro-am golf tournament played annually at The Bear's Club in Jupiter, Florida, in honor of their 17-month-old grandson who drowned in a hot tub in 2005. It has grown to become the foundation's chief fundraiser. No one accepts a fee. Everything goes to the foundation and the organization has raised several million dollars.

Nicklaus and retired General John Shalikashvili, Chairman of the Joint Chiefs of Staff from 1993–97, both serve as honorary chairs for the American Lake Veterans Golf Course capital campaign in Tacoma, WA. Together they raised $4.5 million and designed the nation's only golf course to rehabilitate wounded and disabled veterans.

Over 160 volunteers run the course and Nicklaus donated his design services to finish the last nine holes, now referred to as the "Nicklaus Nine." Nicklaus said, "I was moved to see the amazing efforts at American Lake Veterans Golf Course where our wounded warriors learn to play golf with the help of an incredible army of volunteers."

Nicklaus was named a Global Ambassador for the International Golf Federation in 2008 and was instrumental in bringing golf to the Olympics for the 2016 games.

In 2014, the United States House of Representatives voted to award Nicklaus the Congressional Gold Medal to recognize his service to the nation in promoting excellence and good sportsmanship. Congress stated that Nicklaus' "magnetic personality and unfailing sense of kindness and thoughtfulness have endeared him to millions throughout the world."

#10 Motocross — Ricky Carmichael. Motocross is considered to be one of the most dangerous sports in the world today. Since its inception, the sport has grown to become a magnet for fearless individuals with a passion for proving themselves. Today the sport has branched into many other forms, including Freestyle Motocross, Supermoto, Supercross, Side Jeeps, and Mini Motocross. If you are a motocross enthusiast, chances are there is one athlete that overshadows all others in fitness, athleticism, ability, and preparation — Ricky Carmichael.

Carmichael is known for his success in motocross in the early 2000s, having won the AMA Motocross Championship 450cc class seven times and the AMA Supercross Championship 450cc class five times. He won the 2002 MX Championship without losing a race, the only motocross rider in history to have a perfect season.

His unrivaled successes in motocross gave him the nickname "The GOAT," standing for Greatest of All Time.

#11 Basketball — Michael Jordan is widely regarded as the best basketball player of all-time.

In 1981, Jordan accepted a basketball scholarship to the University of North Carolina, where he played as a Tar Heel under Coach Dean Smith. He was named the NCAA freshman of the year and made the winning shot in the 1982 NCAA Championship game against Georgetown. His Air-ness, as he would later be nicknamed, joined the NBA's Chicago Bulls in 1984, where his global recognition of greatness would skyrocket.

He became the second player, behind Wilt Chamberlain, to score 3,000 points in a season, averaging a league-high 37.1 points on 48.2% shooting. He was the first player in NBA history to record 200 steals and 100 blocks in a season.

Many basketball enthusiasts consider Jordan to be the greatest perimeter scorer in the history of basketball. He dominated the 80s and 90s in both offensive and defensive prowess. Jordan was a nine-time All-Defensive First Team selectee. He was most remembered as a clutch shooter when the game was on the line, and he never lost in the NBA Finals.

Jordan's accolades and accomplishments include five Most Valuable Player (MVP) Awards, ten All-NBA First Team distinctions, nine All-Defensive First Team honors, fourteen NBA All-Star Game appearances, three All-Star Game MVP Awards, ten scoring titles, three steals titles, six NBA Finals MVP Awards, and the 1988 NBA Defensive Player of the Year Award. Among his numerous accomplishments, Jordan holds the NBA records for highest career regular-season scoring average (30.12 points per game) and highest career playoff scoring average (33.45 points per game).

In 1999, ESPN named Jordan the greatest North American athlete of the 20th century. A two-time inductee into the Basketball Hall of Fame, and a member of the men's Olympic Dream Team, Jordan became the first billionaire NBA player in history.

#12 American Football — Jim Brown, Cleveland Browns running back, 1957-1965.

Forty years after his retirement at the peak of his career, and seventh on the all-time rushing list, Brown is still the standard by which all other running backs are measured. His career lasted nine seasons with a 12-game schedule. Considering the relatively brief time he played in the National Football League, he amassed 12,312 rushing yards. His average carry of 5.2-yard is still the highest average among the game's top 20 all-time rushers.

On the gridiron, Brown was a force like no other. His brute force pummeled would-be tacklers, and he consistently outran defenders in the secondary. He was named the greatest professional football player ever by *Sporting News* in 2002.

As a sophomore at Syracuse University (1954), Brown was the second leading rusher on the team. As a junior, he rushed for 666 yards (5.2 per carry). In his senior year, Brown was a unanimous first-team All-American. He finished fifth in the Heisman Trophy voting and set school records for highest season rush average (6.2) and most rushing touchdowns in a single game (6).

Brown left the NFL as the league's all-time leader in rushing touchdowns (106), total touchdowns (126), and most all-purpose yards (15,549). He was the league's first player to reach 100 rushing touchdowns. Brown is the only rusher in NFL history to average over 100 yards per game for his entire career

Following his football career, Brown entered Hollywood and had a successful acting career, appearing in more than 50 movies, television series, and cameo appearances.

 # 13 Boxing — Muhammed Ali, aka Cassius Marcellus Clay Jr. Ali first turned to boxing when he was 12 years of age following an incident in which his bicycle was stolen. He voiced his anger and desire to "Whup" the thief to Louisville Police Officer and boxing trainer Joe Martin. The officer's advice to young Cassius was, "you should first learn how to box." Those words changed the course of boxing history.

That one small interaction was the catalyst that would begin Ali's journey to becoming the "Greatest" boxer of all time. Clay went on to win six Kentucky Golden Gloves titles, two national Golden Gloves titles, one Amateur

Athletic Union National Title, and the Light Heavyweight gold medal in the 1960 Summer Olympics held in Rome, Italy. His amateur record was 100 wins, with just five losses.

In 1962, Clay was introduced to Malcolm X, who would become his spiritual and political mentor. Ali soon became a black activist, airing statements in press conferences such as, "My enemy is the white people, not the Vietcong" and "No intelligent black man or black woman in his or her right black mind wants white boys and white girls coming to their homes to marry their black sons and daughters." At the time, Ali's religious beliefs included the white man was "the devil" and that white people were not "righteous."

At 22 years of age, Ali shocked the world by winning the world heavyweight championship in 1964 by beating Sonny Liston. Shortly thereafter, he joined Islam and changed his name to Muhammed Ali. In 1975, he converted to Sunni Islam. His religious beliefs reached maximum velocity three years later when Ali refused conscript into the U.S. military. Ali cited his religious beliefs and his opposition to America's involvement in the Vietnam War. Thus, he was arrested, tried, and found guilty of draft evasion. As a punishment, Ali was stripped of his boxing title and would live the next four years without a single fight.

Ali appealed to the Supreme Court, and in 1971 his conviction was overturned. As a conscious objector to the Vietnam War, Ali became an iconic figure to anti-war culturalism for generations to come.

As the world's only three-time-lineal heavyweight champion, he won that standing and title in 1964, 1974, and 1978. His most memorable fights were against Sonny Liston, "Smokin" Joe Frazier, and George Foreman.

During an era in which managers spoke for their fighters, Ali took center ring in representing himself, having been inspired by a professional wrestler named George Wagner. Ali craved the media spotlight with no holds barred. He held back no punches when it came to boasting of his greatness. And any polarized political issue was his playground, especially issues related to racial prejudice. As writer Joyce Carol Oates stated, "he was one of the few athletes in sports history to define the terms of his public reputation."

In what has later been called the golden age of heavyweight boxing, Ali defeated every top heavyweight in his era. The Associated Press reported that Ali and Babe Ruth were the two most recognized athletes in America. He appeared on the cover of Sports Illustrated magazine on 37 different occasions, second only to Michael Jordan.

On January 8, 2005, Muhammad Ali received the Presidential Citizens Medal from President George W. Bush. He later received the Presidential Medal of Freedom at a White House ceremony. In 2005, he was awarded the "Otto Hahn Peace Medal in Gold" from the UN Association of Germany for his involvement in the U.S. civil rights movement and the United Nations. Ali received an honorary doctorate of humanities at Princeton University at its 260th graduation ceremony.

In November 2005, the Muhammad Ali Center, a non-profit organization, opened in downtown Louisville. In addition to Ali's boxing memorabilia displays, the center reflects four main principles of peace, social responsibility, respect, and personal growth.

His greatest fight would begin three years following his retirement from boxing, when at age 42 he was diagnosed with Parkinson's Disease, a chronic neuro-disease that attacks nearly every cell in the human body. Ali would battle the disease for almost half his life. He died at age 74 from complications of Parkinson's on June 3, 2016.

 # 14 Badminton — Lin Dan, born in Longyan, Fujian, China, is a two-time Olympic champion, five-time world champion, five-time All England champion, and, to most badminton fans, is recognized as the greatest singles player of all time.

At 28 years of age, he became the only badminton player to complete the "Super Grand Slam" by winning all nine of badminton's major titles (the Olympic Games, the World Championships, the World Cup, the Thomas Cup, the Sudirman Cup, the Super Series, the Masters Finals, the All England Open, the Asian Games, and the Asian Championships). Lin is also the first men's singles player to defend his Olympic title by winning back-to-back gold medals in 2008 and 2012.

Lin's parents wanted their son to learn the piano when he was young, but Lin's interests lead him to badminton when he was only five years old. Scouted by the People's Liberation Army Sports Team, he enlisted into the Chinese National Badminton Team upon winning the National Junior Championships at age 12.

Peter Gade, a well-known badminton opponent, referred to Lin as "Super Dan" in 2004 when they faced each other in the All England Open Final. The nickname has remained with Lin ever since.

In 2012, he received a master's degree from Huaqiao University, becoming the first active Chinese badminton player to do so. His biography, *Until the End of the World*, was published soon after he won the 2012 Olympic title.

#15 Running – Before each of these previous sports, or perhaps any sport was conceived, there was running. The mystique behind long-distance running is endurance. What is it that allows a runner to withstand hardship or adversity, especially while in the midst of a prolonged stressful circumstance or activity? Marathon runners are well acquainted with this definition. The training, nutritional, physical, and especially the mental preparation and stamina it takes to complete a marathon can be enormous.

George Sheehan, born in Brooklyn, New York, understood well the requirements of becoming an endurance runner. The eldest of 14 children, Sheehan began running at an early age. As a student at Manhattan College, he honed his craft meticulously and became a college icon in running.

Sheehan began writing about running and became the editor for *Runners World* in 1970, where he became a columnist for two decades. The popularity of the articles he wrote turned *Runners World* into the number one magazine in running. Sheehan authored eight books about running and living life to the fullest. He continued running until his legs gave out with his final book, *Going the Distance*, written on the process of dying. Sheehan exemplified the value of living an active and fulfilling life, and above all, Be Authentic."

Sheehan was an expert on endurance and mental tenacity it took to be a world-class runner. His philosophy on endurance was simple, "It's extremely hard, in the beginning, to understand that the whole idea is not to beat the other runners. Eventually, you learn that the competition is against the little voice inside you that wants you to quit."

The Ultra-Sports Achievers

Most participants who compete in Ultra-Sports are from a different universe than our own. They either have a mutual disrespect for mediocrity or a disregard for their human bodies. What characteristics are requisite for an Ultra-Athlete to compete in these events? How do these ferocious competitors achieve the degree of success they enjoy in showcasing their amazing athletic skills?

What forms the abilities of these celestial-like overachievers? Genetics, aptitude, and athleticism may qualify as the entrance fees. But mental toughness, tenacity, endurance, and the sheer will to overcome challenges and obstacles are far beyond the average person's born traits.

If you are like me, many of these competitions may be unfamiliar and even unfathomable to you until you read about them. Even if you have heard of some of these competitions, it is highly probable that you would be hard pressed to name the champions within the events.

The Bad Water Ultramarathon was established in 2002 by Al Arnold, founder and the first inductee to the Bad Water Hall of Fame. Arnold became the first man to complete the event in 1977. The run begins at Death Valley, California, the lowest point in the United States at 280 feet below sea level. It ends at the trailhead of Mount Whitney, the highest summit in the Continental United States.

The Bad Water competition covers 135 miles of running and occurs in summer temperatures that can reach above 130 degrees Fahrenheit. During the event, the asphalt can reach 200 degrees requiring runners to stay on the white painted lines to keep their shoes from melting! Runners are drenched with ice water every 15 minutes to lower their body temperatures and prevent heat exhaustion.

Marshal Ulrich has the most wins in the men's category, having won the race in 1991, 1992, 1993, and 1996. Jamie Donaldson and Judy Overholtzer have each won three consecutive years in the women's competition. Overholtzer took home the trophy in 1994, 1995, and 1996. Donaldson won the competition in 2008, 2009, and 2010. Pete Kostelnick holds the course record at a sizzling pace of 21:56:32 that equates to 9.75 minutes per mile.

The Barkley Marathons are divided into two races, a 100 mile (160 km) run and a 60 mile (97 km) "fun run." The races are held annually in Head State Park near Wartburg, Tennessee, in late March and early April. Runners in the 100 Mile competition circle a 20-mile loop five times, with loops three and four run in the opposite direction and loop five at the runner's choice. Modeled after a prison escape, runners cover 65,000 feet of vertical climbing through five 20-mile unmarked loops. Runners in the 100-mile race must finish the race within 60 hours. The distance and grade are the equivalent of climbing Mt. Everest twice in three days.

The race has had only 16 runners complete the course in the allotted time since 1986. That is about a 1% chance of success ratio for a new entrant. Brian Robinson set the course record in 2008, posting the current world record time of 55 hours, 42 minutes and 27 seconds with an average speed of about 33.42 minutes per mile.

The Dragon's Back Race is the world's longest five-day mountain race in the world. It spans 200 miles with an ascension of 47,770 feet. The race covers the entire length of Wales, beginning at Conway Castle in the north and ending at Carreg Cennen Castle in the south.

In 1992 Helen Diamantides and Martin Stone entered the record books. Competing against many of the great ultra-runners from around the globe, they posted a winning time of 38 hours and 38 minutes in Dragon's Back's inaugural race. The pair averaged a speed of about 11.59 miles per hour.

Diamantides, a phenomenal runner, would go on to set many other world records. In 1987, she beat the world record for running from Everest Base Camp to Kathmandu, 167 miles with 32,000 feet of ascent and 46,000 feet of descent in 3 days and 10 hours (with eight hours of sleep in between).

The Iditarod Trail Invitational (ITI) was founded in 2002 and is currently the world's longest winter ultramarathon. Athletes compete by mountain bike, foot, and skis. Following the historic Iditarod Trail that begins in Knik, Alaska, passes over the Alaska Range to McGrath, and ends in Nome, Alaska, the event is held in late February, one week before the famed Iditarod Trail Sled Dog Race.

The ITI differs from most races in that the founders felt it was important to let racers make their own decisions about what they should carry, when to rest, and what safety precautions they should consider. The ITI has no designated trails or marked routes; only mandatory checkpoints racers must pass through during the race.

Course records vary from as few as ten days up to as many as 17 days, depending on weather conditions. In 2012, due to adverse weather, not a single rider completed the race. Mitch Seavey currently has the fastest time, completing the race in 8 days, 3 hours, 40 minutes, and 15 seconds. Libby Riddles was the first woman to win the race in 1985, and Rick Swenson holds the record for most wins at five.

The Iron Man Competition was created during an award ceremony following a Hawaiian running race. Navy Commander John Collins and several of the competitors debated what type of athlete is more fit. Collins suggested a race that included swimming, cycling, and running would answer the question. "Whoever finishes first, we'll call the Ironman," said Collins, and thus the "Ironman Triathlon" was born.

Today's, Ironman competition is held each year in Kona, Hawaii. Competitors must complete a 2.4-mile swim, 112-mile bike ride, and a full 26.2-mile marathon. To be considered an "Ironman," the competitor must stay within the following time cutoffs: swimming (2 hours 20 minutes), cycling (8 hours 10 minutes), and marathon (6 hours 30 minutes). The recommended training regimen to prepare for the event is seven swimming miles per week, 232 cycling miles per week, and 48 running miles per week.

In summary, if you have what it takes to compete at world-class times in three widely different and extremely taxing athletic disciplines, giving all the physical and mental focus you can muster, and sustain that energy for 17 hours straight in temperatures that may exceed 105 degrees, then you too can be called an Ironman. The record time is held by Mark Allen, a six-time champion who completed the race in an astounding time of 8:07:46.

The La Ruta de Los Conquistadores begins in the high-altitude peaks of the Costa Rican jungle and takes the rider from the Pacific Ocean to the Atlantic Ocean. Cyclists must navigate knee-deep mud and sand over four riding stages, climbing a total of 29,000 feet over 161 miles.

The competitors in this race accomplish in three days what it took the Spanish Conquistadors to accomplish in 20 years. The ride is physically demanding and mentally draining. It is also potentially hazardous to your health because of the poisonous dart frogs the competitors encounter along the way. As you might expect, due to the distance and climbing involved, riders might need a few days to complete the race. Federico Ramirez, a five-time winner of the race, has crossed the finishing line with a blistering pace of just over 12 hours.

The Marathon des Sables celebrated its 30-year anniversary in 2015. The race is popular and averages about 1300 entrants, including 200+ women. Arguably the most difficult footrace in the world, the event takes runners across 150 miles of Moroccan desert (the equivalent of 5.5 marathons) carrying food and supplies strapped to their backs and running in temperatures exceeding 125 degrees. The race has several stages with water stations strategically situated along the way to allow the runners to hydrate themselves.

In 1994, a runner named Mauro Prosperi was lost in a sandstorm and wandered the Moroccan desert alone for approximately 125 miles. Prosperi survived the ordeal by eating bats and drinking his own urine to survive. Eventually, he was found, having trimmed his weight by 30 pounds. Moroccan brothers Lahcen and Mohamad Ahansal have the most wins, with ten races between the two.

The Race Across America (RAAM) was first known as The Great American Bike Race. This cycling event, considered the toughest endurance race in the world, was established in 1982 by a rider named John Marino. The race begins in Oceanside, California and ends in Annapolis, Maryland. Riders pedal 3000 miles and climb more than 170,000 feet through deserts, plains, mountains, and valleys. Over 2,000 cyclists have competed in RAAM since 1982. Top competitors average 22 hours a day and 250 to

350 miles of cycling. The race has a 12-day limit to complete to receive credit. The shortest qualifying round is 375 miles long.

In 2006, the rules of the race were altered primarily for safety reasons. Solo riders were required to rest for a total of 40 hours at pre-selected points across the country to mitigate the emphasis on sleep deprivation and turn the focus toward long-distance riding speeds. The world record holder is Christopher Strasser, who rode 3020 miles in 2014, maintaining an average of 16.42 mph and crossing the finish line in a remarkable time of 7 days, 15 hours, and 56 minutes.

The Self-Transcendence is the longest certified footrace in the world and was dubbed the Mount Everest of Ultramarathons by the New York Times. Competitors must have enormous courage, physical stamina, extreme focus, and the ability to endure fatigue, boredom, and injury. The 3100-mile running course consists of a single block in a corner of Queens, New York. Runners average 59.6 miles per day on concrete sidewalks, passing a playground, ball fields, and within the confines of a vocational high school in a neighborhood setting. Runners must complete the race in 52 days, equivalent to 5,649 laps.

In the past 18 years, there have been 37 runners that have completed the race. The current record was set in 2006 by Madhupran Wolfgang Schwerk, who completed the event in 41 days, eight hours, shattering his previous record by 29 hours. Suprabha Beckjord won 10 straight Self-Transcendence events in a row.

The Tour de France, established in 1903, is a three-week endurance bicycle race spanning 2,200 miles. It concludes on the final day of competition at the Arc de Triomphe in Paris. The ride typically occurs in July and comprises nine stages of level terrain, four medium mountain stages, five steeper mountain stages, and two trial stages. The ride passes through the Pyrenees and the Swiss Alps mountain regions. The rider who maintains the lowest aggregate time gets to don the "Yellow Jersey," a symbol that he is the leader and rider to beat.

One of the more prolific riders of the race, Eddy Merck, earned the title of King of the Mountains when he won the combination classification, combative award, and the points competition, all in the same year. The year was 1969, and it was his first race on the circuit!

The Tour Divide is a 2,745-mile course that takes trail bikers from the Rocky Mountains in Canada to the Mexican border. It runs from Banff to New Mexico and features dirt roads, jeep trails, unpredictable high-altitude weather, and blazing heat. It is an extremely difficult ride, even for a seasoned competitor. Riders may pedal 170 miles per day and climb more than 200,000 vertical feet.

The 2014 winner finished the race in 16 days, 2 hours, and 39 minutes. To break it down, the Tour Divide equals 12,500 feet of climbing per day for 16 days straight. Josh Kato, the men's record holder, completed the race in June 2015 in 14 days, 11 hours, and 37 minutes. Lael Wilcox is the female record holder, finishing with a time of 17 days, 1 hour, and 51 minutes.

The Ultra-Trail du Mont-Blanc directs runners across three countries: France, Italy, and Switzerland. Overflowing with scenery, this high-altitude, 103-mile tour of the Alps must be finished in 46 hours or less. Top finishers complete the race in less than 20 hours. The mountain race takes runners to an altitude of 8200 feet amidst the darkness of night and wind, cold, rain, or snow. The 2014 winner of this event was Francois D'haene of

France, finishing in a time of 20 hours, 11 minutes, and 44 seconds.

The Volvo Ocean Race, held once every three years, is a yacht competition spanning 38,739 nautical miles crossing four oceans and five continents. The world's longest sporting event pits teams of eight (eleven for all-women teams) for nine months spread over nine or ten legs.

Crews race throughout the day and night, for up to 20 consecutive days on some legs. Teams include two sailors with medical training, one sailmaker, an engineer, and a media crewman. Meals are all freeze-dried, and temperatures may vary from a low of 23 degrees Fahrenheit to a high of 104 degrees Fahrenheit.

The Climb

There is one ultra-marathon that few of us, if any, are unfamiliar. There is a high probability that you can name the first duo to accomplish the feat in 1953.

The Ultra Event that I am referring to has captivated the interest and respect of people around the globe. It is a challenge that demands the utmost physical stamina, mental alertness, strength, emotional courage, and it inspires a spiritual reverence.

This Ultra-Event is the apex of endurance and difficulty. The harshness of the achievement is reflected by the many human body markers along the journey of those who fell short of their destination. The event I am referring to has simply come to be known as "The Climb."

Mount Everest is referred to by the Nepalese as Sagarmatha, which means "Head of the Sky." At 29,029 feet in height, this three-sided pyramid-shaped mountain is the tallest mountain above sea level in the world. The north and east side is in Tibet, and its southwest side is in Nepal.

Until 1920, Tibet did not allow outsiders to climb the mountain. But in 1921, through much persuasion, climbers were allowed access. Today's route through Nepal is called the North Ridge and has become the preferred route used by climbing teams.

The dangers of ascending Mount Everest are many. First, as a person moves higher, oxygen levels drop, and pressure increases. Second, climbers face dangerous ice falls, the most challenging being called the "Khumbu" where 19 people have died while crossing. Third, extreme weather can cause exhaustion, frostbite, and situations where climbers have slipped and fallen to their death on the frozen ground beneath.

More than 4000 climbers have summited the mountain since Hillary and Mallory (as you probably already knew) became the first to reach the top on May 29th, 1953. And more than 200 have died in the attempt since. With a 5% chance of death, you might risk the odds for the bragging rights, but if you were to fly on an airline that you knew had one fatal crash every 20 flights would you board the plane?

The accomplishment of Hillary and Mallory is remarkable, considering they wore wool, cotton, and leather as compared with today's advanced synthetic materials that weigh 70% less. Their axes were wooden and heavy compared to today's light aluminum axes. Their sleeping bags and tents were three times heavier. And their food was fish and fruit stored in metal tins rather than today's energy bars and electrolyte shots.

In 1997, author Jon Krakauer wrote a best-selling book, *Into Thin Air*, a narrative about the 1996 ascent of Mount Everest when a rogue storm killed eight climbers and stranded several others. What was the driving force that motivated these men and women to embark on such a journey? To answer that question, let us first consider the mountain they chose and the difficulty of the ascent.

To reach the summit of Mt. Everest, a climber begins at base camp and then works their way up the mountain, stopping at five camps along the ascent, each located at a significant altitude higher than the previous camp. Besides the altitude adjustments, which is a major concern, each camp is within an average climber's ability. Each camp is used as an acclimation point to allow the climber to adjust to the thinning air.

Beyond camp five, the climb becomes technically challenging. Camp VI is hardly a camp at all, but rather a small niche of limited safety from the obstacles above. The crescendo of the climb is a series of technical walls approaching the summit referred to as the first, second, and third steps.

The second step is the hardest of the three and is called the Hillary Step. A cautious climbing technique is often used at this point of the ascension called a Z-System (a configuration of rope, anchors, and pulleys typically used to extricate a climber after falling into a crevasse).

As with most of the highest mountains around the world, there is a drop-dead recommended turnaround time from the summit to allow for a safe return. For Mount Everest, that time is generally considered to be 2:00 PM.

The urge to be "the first" in summiting Mount Everest was powerful. The feat was finally accomplished in 1953 by Sir Edmund Hillary and Tenzing Norgay when they became the first to reach the summit and stand at the top of the world. Everything since then has been, well, second.

Not to be deterred at the thought of being second, there have been all manner of attempts since 1953 at other "Everest firsts." These include the first to paraglide off Everest, the first to ski down Everest, the first blind person to climb Everest, and other milestones.

In 2013, Japanese climber Yuichiro Miura, at age 80, became the oldest person to climb and reach the top of Everest. He had summited Everest twice before. Even more remarkable than his age is that he had survived four heart operations, and in 2009 he broke his pelvis while skiing. A former extreme skier, Miura commented that while the ascent was difficult, the descent nearly killed him.

Here are just a few other noteworthy accomplishments:

- The first solo ascent: Reinhold Messner on August 20, 1980.

- The first oxygen-less ascent: Reinhold Messer on May 8, 1979.

- The youngest person to summit Everest: Jordan Romero on May 22, 2010 (13 years of age).

- Aba Sherpa has made it to the summit of Everest 21 times.

- In May of 2016, Charlie Linville, a retired U.S. Marine Corp Staff Sargent, became the first combat-wounded veteran to summit Mount Everest. It was his third attempt, having failed to reach the summit in 2014 and 2015.

Numerous deterrents face those who want to climb Mt. Everest. First and foremost are the financial constraints. Climbing Mt. Everest can cost climbers their entire nest eggs. The Licensing and Permit Fee is $11,000. The Life

Insurance policy costs $15,000. The Sherpa Guide Fee is mandatory and ranges from local guides at a minimum of $4,000 to Western Guides that can cost $10,000 to $25,000. Full package deals with Western Guides can run upwards of $60.000.

A second major consideration is the extensive time commitment to training. Plus, there is the risk of life and limb while knowing you may not even reach the top. For most, the opportunity cost would direct us toward a lesser financial and time-consuming endeavor, and certainly one that is less life threatening.

So now we can look back at our earlier question, "What was the driving force that motivated these men and women to spend exorbitant sums of money, push themselves beyond physical limitations, and to risk life and limb? The following reasons were shared by those few that have successfully summited the top of the world:

1) The Challenge? "Because it was there," said Sir Edmund Hillary, the first person to reach the summit (in 1953).

2) The Awe of the Experience? "The highest of the world's mountains, it seems, has to make but a single gesture of magnificence to be the lord of all, vast in unchallenged and isolated supremacy," according to George Mallory, who reached the summit with Hillary.

3) To Achieve the Pinnacle of Climbing Success? "The end of the ridge and the end of the world...then nothing but that clear, empty air. There was nowhere else to climb. I was standing on the top of the world," said Stacy Allison, the first American woman to reach the summit of Everest.

4) Self-Realization? "Mountains are not fair or unfair; they are just dangerous. I am nothing more than a single narrow gasping lung, floating over the mists and summits." ~ Reinhold Messner

5) Mind over Matter? "Technique and ability alone do not get you to the top; it is the willpower that is the most important. This willpower you cannot buy with money or be given by others...it rises from your heart." ~ Junko Tabei, the first woman to climb Everest, in 1975.

6) Courage beyond limits? "We agreed that this was going to be no ordinary climb. For the time being, Everest was rather more than a mountain." ~ John Hunt, the 1953 expedition leader for Hillary and Mallory.

7) Reaching beyond physical boundaries? "Everest for me, and I believe for the world, is the physical and symbolic manifestation of overcoming odds to achieve a dream." ~ Tom Whittaker, the first disabled person to climb Mt. Everest.

CHAPTER 6

The Spiritual Rulers

Faith, hope, charity, and compassion are the driving virtues that foster selflessness, sacrifice, and humanitarian causes of all kinds in communities, countries, and homes around the world. The individuals who envision, facilitate, and perpetuate these causes are religious and spiritual leaders.

Throughout history, spiritual leaders have endured criticism, opposition, and adversity of every kind for their convictions and beliefs. The principles and doctrines they professed, the courage they exhibited, and the passionate vigor they personified in carrying out their missions is an attraction and inspiration to their followers and an ensign to the world of their commitment to the causes in which they were engaged. Passionate to the point of death (PTTPOD). These faithful and courageous men and women gave all that they possessed, even life itself, in defense of their beliefs. Their lives have become a standard of nobility and a testament of greatness for those that follow them.

The origins of these spiritual rulers and the religious legacies they built generally hold at least one of the following common threads. They were students or successors to a religiously notable predecessor; they were inspired to correct or purify an existing religious norm. They were heavenly directed to follow a different path. They were known by a specific title such as reformer, prophet, evangelist, or saint. Their teachings of inspiration, ideas, or God's word are compiled in one or more texts.

The courageous and passionate visionaries and ministers of change you will read about possessed the bravery and conviction to break away from the religious mainstream and common beliefs of the communities in which they were raised. They also possessed the oratory skills, passion, and charisma to convince others to follow them. The religions they established, and their contributions to the causes they represented, have weathered the test of time, while leaving legacies for their followers to build upon.

The Changing Face of Religion Today
The religious profile of the world is rapidly changing, driven primarily by differences in fertility rates, the size of youth populations among the world's major religions, and people switching faiths.

As of 2010, Christianity was the world's largest religion by far, with an estimated 2.2 billion adherents, nearly a third (31%) of all 6.9 billion people on Earth. Islam was second, with 1.6 billion adherents, or 23% of the global population.

Over the next four decades, Christians will remain the largest religious group, but Islam will grow faster than any other major religion. As a result, the projected size disparity between Muslims and Christians will be less than 100 million. At current growth rates, there will be 2.8 billion Islamic followers by 2050, or 30% of the world population, and 2.9 billion Christians, or 31% of the world population.

If current trends continue, the Pew Research Center forecasts that by 2050:

- The number of Muslims will nearly equal the number of Christians around the world.

- Atheists, agnostics, and other people who do not affiliate with any religion, though increasing in countries such as the United States and France, will make up a declining share of the world's total population.

- The global Buddhist population will be about the same size it was in 2010, while the Hindu and Jewish populations will become larger.

- In Europe, Muslims will comprise 10% of the overall population.

- While India will retain a Hindu majority, it will also have the largest Muslim population of any country in the world, surpassing Indonesia.

- In the United States, Christians will decline from more than three-quarters of the population in 2010 to two-thirds in 2050. Judaism will no longer be the largest non-Christian religion. Muslims will be more numerous in the U.S. than people who identify as Jewish.

- Four out of every 10 Christians in the world will live in sub-Saharan Africa.

The unbridled bandwidth of today's wireless Internet affords spiritual leaders a voice and a platform for spreading their messages almost instantaneously. Through social media, religious leaders and organizations can reach millions, and even billions, of supporters around the world. In less than 150 years, spreading the word has gone from a local event to a worldwide phenomenon. With modern-day telecommunications networks able to bridge vast distances across the globe, religion is no longer constrained by physical boundaries.

It would take several volumes to list all the spiritual and inspirational leaders that have impacted and reformed religion and beliefs since Adam and Eve. For the purposes of this chapter, we will refer only to individuals that left a global imprint on society and a lasting legacy worthy of a noble and great one, personified by their commitment to their causes and their concerns for humanity. These spiritual leaders' lives have touched millions. They are among the most recognized and influential spiritual leaders in the world throughout history. Volumes have been written about the deeds and accomplishments of these unique and remarkable leaders. Unfortunately, we will only have space for a brief synopsis of these gifted individuals.

Now let us take a closer look at just a few of the spiritual leaders responsible for establishing these religions and the doctrines they teach. Listed in alphabetical order, they are as follows:

Confucius — a Chinese spiritual leader whose teachings were based on ethics and morality. He mostly taught about modesty, respect, honesty, and sincerity.

Confucius was a strong proponent of living a good life. Confucianism has been thought of as a system of social and ethical philosophies rather than a mainstream religion. Confucianism is woven into Chinese culture as a way of life. To Confucians, life itself is the stage of religion.

Confucianism built on an ancient religious foundation to establish the social values, institutions, and transcendent ideals of traditional Chinese society. Sociologist Robert Bellah called Confucianism a "civil religion."

Confucianism brought identity and common moral understanding to the foundations of a society's central institutions. It is also what one Chinese sociologist called a "diffused religion" as its institutions are not a separate church, but those of society, family, school, and state. Its priests are not separate liturgical specialists, but parents, teachers, and officials. The objective of Confucianism is to establish social values, institutions, and transcendent ideals for traditional Chinese society.

Confucius embraced Humaneness through *Ren*, translated to mean love or kindness, the source of all virtues. The Chinese character for Ren represents the relationship between "two persons," or co-humanity. *Ren* keeps ritual forms from becoming hollow; a ritual performed with *ren* has ethical content; it nurtures the person's inner character, furthering his or her ethical maturation. The "outer" side of Confucianism is conformity of social roles, while the "inner" side represents conscience and character. Cultivation involves education and self-inspection. Confucianism has been compared to carving and polishing the stone of one's character until it is a lustrous gem.

Gendün Drupa — the first Dalai Lama of Tibetan Buddhism. He lived from 1391 to 1474. Drupa was born in a cowshed in Gyurmey Rupa near Sakya in the region of central Tibet. Raised as a shepherd until the age of seven, he took his Sramanera (novitiate) vows from the abbot of Narthang, Khenchen Drupa Sherap, in 1405.

At 20 years old, he received the name Gedun Drupa upon taking the vows of a bhikṣu (monk) from the abbot of Narthang Monastery and became a student of the scholar and reformer Je Tonkawa (1357–1419), who some say was his uncle. Around this time, he also became the first abbot of Ganden Monastery, founded by Tsongkhapa himself in 1409. By the middle of his life, Drupa had become one of the most esteemed scholar-saints in the country.

Tradition states that Palden Lhamo, the female guardian spirit of the sacred lake, Lhamo La-tso, promised the First Dalai Lama in one of his visions "...that she would protect the reincarnation lineage of the Dalai Lamas." Since the time of Gedun Gyatso, who formalized the system, monks have gone to the lake to meditate when seeking visions with guidance on finding the next reincarnation.

Drupa founded the major monastery of Tashilhunpo at Shigatse. He remained the abbot of Tashilhunpo Monastery until he died while meditating in 1474 at the age of 83.

The Samding Dorje Phagmo (1422–1455), the highest female incarnation in Tibet, was a contemporary of Gedun Drupa. Her teacher, the Bodongpa Panchen Chogley Namgyal, was also one of his teachers; he received many teachings and empowerments from him.

Some of the most famous texts Drupa wrote were *Sunlight on the Path to Freedom*, a commentary on Abhidharma-kosa; *Crushing the Forces of Evil to Dust*, an epic poem on the life and liberating deeds of Gautama Buddha; *Song of the Eastern Snow Mountain*, a poem dedicated to Je Tsongkhapa; and *Praise of the Venerable Lady Khadiravani Tara*, an homage to Tara.

Gautama Buddha – lived between the 5th to 4th century BCE. He was born into an upper-class family that was part of the Shakya clan. In his 45-year ministry, he became one of the most prolific individuals in the history of India.

Buddha was known as a philosopher, mendicant, meditator, and spiritual teacher. Also referred to as the enlightened one, Buddha was believed to have transcended above Karma and escaped the cycle of *Samsara*, the mechanism which keeps people trapped in the cycle of rebirth. According to the Oxford online dictionary, Hinduism and Buddhism teach the sum of a person's actions in this and previous states of existence decide their fate in future existences.

Buddhism teaches there are Four Noble Truths of suffering. First, there is a cause of suffering. Second, suffering has an end. Third, there is a true path that leads to the end of suffering. Fourth, the cause of suffering is to bring about its end. More simply put, suffering exists; it has a cause; it has an end, and its cause is to bring about its end.

Buddha traveled throughout the Ganges Plain, teaching and building a religious community. His teaching was based on his insight into *duḥkha*, which is the word for suffering and reaching a state of being known as *Nibbāna* or *Nirvana*. The Buddha religion teaches self-denial and self-discipline. Buddha taught there is a spiritual path that included ethical behavior, meditative practices, and being mindful of self and others.

It also refers to the spiritual principle of cause and effect where an individual's intent and actions (cause) influence the future of that individual (effect). Good intent and good deeds contribute to good karma and happier rebirths, while bad intent and bad deeds contribute to bad karma and bad rebirths.

Jesus Christ of Nazareth - there is no religious leader more influential than Jesus Christ. He lived between 7 to 36 CE and has impacted billions of followers worldwide and the course of history throughout the ages. Over 2000 years since his death, his spiritual teachings are still followed, reverenced, and revered.

Known by more than 600 names and titles, and 400 prophesies chronicling His pre-mortal life, His birth, His purpose here in mortality, His Atonement, His betrayal by one of His disciples, Judas Iscarius, His infamous sentencing by an unjust and unholy mob comprised of His own religious family, His death, His triumphant return, His banishment of Lucifer and his minions, and His triumphant return to rule and reign upon the earth are all testaments to His nobility and greatness.

The life of Jesus Christ was documented in the *Holy Bible*, the most read religious text in Christianity, with at least five billion copies sold and translated into 700 languages as of September 2020. *Christ* (a Greek word) and *Messiah* (a Hebrew word) mean "the anointed." Jesus Christ is the Firstborn of the Father in the spirit (Hebrews 1:6; Doctrine and Covenants 93:21). He is the Only Begotten of the Father in the flesh (John 1:14; 3:16). He is Jehovah (Doctrine and Covenants 110:3–4) and was foreordained to His great calling before the creation of the world.

Jesus was born to Mary in Bethlehem, lived a sinless life, and made a perfect atonement for the sins of all mankind by the shedding of His blood and giving His life on the cross (Matthew 2:1; 1 Nephi 11:13-33; 3 Nephi 27:13-16; Doctrine and Covenants 76:40-42). He rose from the dead, thus assuring the eventual resurrection of all mankind.

Through Jesus' Atonement and Resurrection, those who repent their sins and obey God's commandments can live eternally with Jesus and the Father. (2 Nephi 9:10–12; 21–22; Doctrine and Covenants 76:50–53, 62).

None other has had so profound an influence upon all who have lived and will yet live upon the earth. He was the Great Jehovah of the Old Testament, the Messiah of the New Testament.

Under the direction of His Father, He was the creator of the earth. "All things were made by him; and without him was not anything made that was made." (John 1:3) Though sinless, He was baptized to fulfill all righteousness. He "went about doing good" (Acts 10:38), yet was despised for it.

His gospel was a message of peace, love, and becoming like His Father who sent Him. He entreated all to follow His example. He walked the roads of Palestine, healing the sick, causing the blind to see, and raising the dead. He taught the truths of eternity, the reality of our premortal existence, the purpose of our life on earth, and the potential for the sons and daughters of God in the life to come. He instituted the sacrament as a reminder of His great atoning sacrifice for all mankind.

According to the prophecy of Isaiah the Prophet, "He was despised and rejected of men; a man of sorrows, and acquainted with grief: and we hid as it were our faces from him; he was despised, and we esteemed him not. Surely he hath borne our griefs, and carried our sorrows: yet we did esteem him stricken, smitten of God, and afflicted." (Isaiah 53:3)

But he was wounded for our transgressions, he was bruised for our iniquities, the chastisement of our peace was upon him, and with his stripes we are healed. His pre-mortal, mortal, and post-mortal life was rejected, betrayed, and condemned by His own people. He was falsely accused by self-righteous hypocrites, who broke their own laws and abandoned any morals left within themselves to sentence a just, honorable, and perfect son of God by exonerating a criminal.

This beloved Son of God, as he willingly hung on the cross at Golgotha, with a broken heart and bowels full of mercy, used His last breath in mortality to petition His Father's forgiveness on behalf of His executioners as he cried out saying, "Father, forgive them, for they do not know what they are doing." (Luke 23:35) And they divided up his clothes by casting lots.

His life was a testament to His desire to please His Father in Heaven and bless the lives of His children. No Father on earth or in heaven will ever be more pleased with a son than the Father was for His Son Jesus. He embodied, emulated, and perfected his gifts and talents to perfection. He was in full command of His emotions, His mental and physical faculties, His spirituality, His intellect, His location, and where he was heading. He showed all mankind how to assess any situation or circumstance in a healthy manner. The depths he has suffered and the jubilation He has experienced make Jesus Christ the Noblest and Greatest individual that has or will ever live on earth or in the heavens.

The prophet Isaiah could not have prophesied more succinctly, "For unto us a child is born, unto us a son is given, and the government shall be upon his shoulder: and his name shall be called Wonderful, Counsellor, The

mighty God, The everlasting Father, The Prince of Peace."
(Isaiah 8:6)

John Calvin — born in 1509, Calvin was a powerful
French theologian and pastor. He was one of the most
revered figures of the Protestant Reform movement in
sixteenth-century Europe.

Although he is considered the successor to German
reformer Martin Luther, he was an independent thinker.
His doctrine, known as Calvinism, differed largely from
Luther's. He came in contact with Renaissance humanism
while studying law at the University of Bourges. It
influenced him so much that he decided to devote his life
to its propagation.

Calvin is best remembered for his reform works. During
his tenure, Geneva grew into a center of Protestantism. He
was also the inspiration behind the establishment of
Presbyterianism in Scotland, the Puritan Movement in
England, and the Reformed Church in the Netherlands.

Calvin wrote a seminal work entitled *Institutio
Christianae Religionis* (Institutes of the Christian
Religion). First published in 1536 in Latin, it was updated
several times by Calvin. Today, it is widely read by
theological students for references on the doctrines
adopted by the Reformed churches.

He also proposed a wide range of disciplinary actions.
These covered everything from the abolition of Roman
Catholic superstition to taking steps against dancing,
gambling, swearing, and enforcement of sexual morality
and the regulation of taverns. He was known for his strict
discipline, punishing dissent or impiety with execution.
Fifty-eight people were executed and 76 were exiled for
their religious beliefs within the first five years of his rule
in Geneva.

Today, the theological traditions practiced by John Calvin and other theologians of that era are known as Calvinism. It is now a major branch of Protestantism, known as Reformed tradition, Reformed Christianity, Reformed Protestantism, or the Reformed Faith. Calvin is recognized as a Renewer of the Church in Lutheran churches and as a saint in both the Church of England and the Episcopal Church in the United States.

Joseph Smith, Jr — recognized and heralded by members of the Church of Jesus Christ of Latter-Day Saints as the Lord's foreordained prophet of the restoration of the fullness of times, preparatory to the second coming of Jesus Christ to rule and reign over the house of Israel forever.

"Joseph Smith, the Prophet and Seer of the Lord, has done more, save Jesus only, for the salvation of men in this world, than any other man that ever lived in it. In the short space of twenty years, he has brought forth the Book of Mormon, which he translated by the gift and power of God, and has the means of publishing it on two continents; has sent the fullness of the everlasting gospel, which it contained, to the four quarters of the earth; has brought forth the revelations and commandments which compose this book of Doctrine and Covenants, and many other wise documents and instructions for the benefit of the children of men; gathered many thousands of the Latter-day Saints, founded a great city, and left a fame and name that cannot be slain. He lived great, and he died great in the eyes of God and his people; and like most of the Lord's anointed in ancient times, has sealed his mission and his works with his own blood; and so has his brother Hyrum. In life they were not divided, and in death they were not separated!" (Doctrine & Covenants 135:3)

Born on December 23, 1805, in the town of Sharon, Windsor County, Vermont, Smith was foreordained and influenced by God to live a very atypical life, an understatement for what he accomplished in the brief span of his 39 years of mortal life.

In 1830, Smith and a few dozen followers established The Church of Jesus Christ of Latter-day Saints, a restoration of the original church founded by Jesus Christ based upon Apostles, Prophets, Seers, and Revelators with Jesus Christ as the chief cornerstone.

Today, The Church of Jesus Christ of Latter-Day Saints is headquartered in Salt Lake City, Utah, and has established congregations in 139 countries with nearly 20 million members and more than 10,000 welfare missionaries. It has over 67,000 members serving in full-time missions, 139 temples in service, four universities, more than 5,000 family history centers, and some 400 thousand students enrolled in Seminary. In 2012, the National Council of Churches ranked The Church of Jesus Christ of Latter-Day Saints as the fourth-largest Christian denomination in the United States.

Krishna — Krishna is regarded as the founder of Hinduism. Hindus comprise the third largest religion, with over 1.25 billion followers, or 15–16% of the global population.

Followers of this religion regard Krishna as part human being, part deity. He is believed to be a reincarnation of the Hindu god Vishnu. Krishna is an inspiration to millions of followers, in part because of his personality traits that reflect righteousness, flamboyance, cheerfulness, serenity, and above all, divinity. Born on earth as an avatar of Lord Vishnu, Krishna lived life like a commoner blessed with divine power. Each God in Hinduism has a unique aura, and so does Krishna. Approximately 80% of Hindus live in India. The only country rivaling this per capita concentration is Nepal, with 23 million followers.

Martin Luther — was born in Eisleben, Saxony, Germany, then a part of the Holy Roman Empire. He is one of the most influential figures in the history of Christianity.

Luther is often referred to as the father of the reformation. He believed that "Next to the word of God, the noble art of music is the greatest treasure in the world."

Luther is also recognized as the founding father of Protestantism. His spiritual journey began as a Catholic priest, where he became disillusioned in many of the church's systems and practices. Feeling that he could do so much more for the welfare of God's children, he began a movement that today is known as Protestantism.

Luther sparked the Protestant Reformation, which began as an attempt to reform the Roman Catholic Church. He challenged the authority of the papacy and attempted to reform certain Christian doctrines through his writings. In addition, his hymns inspired the development of congregational singing within Christianity.

He translated the Bible from Hebrew and ancient Greek into the German language, which made the Scriptures more accessible to the common man, leading to a tremendous impact on the church and German culture. His translations helped in popularizing Christianity and aided the development of a standard version of the German language.

Luther authored *The 95 Theses,* which is widely regarded as the initial catalyst for the Protestant Reformation. The theses questioned the Catholic Church's practice of selling indulgences and protested clerical abuses, especially nepotism, simony, usury, and pluralism.

Recanting several of his Catholic beliefs, Luther proceeded to reformulate some basic tenets of Christian belief that resulted in Western Christendom's division into two factions: Roman Catholicism and the newly formed Protestant traditions.

Pope Leo X and the Holy Roman Emperor Charles V were angered by Luther's actions and asked him to retract all his writings. He refused to do so and was excommunicated by the pope.

His rebellious actions against the theologies and practices of the most powerful religion in Christendom were a testament to his faith, courage, and commitment.

He stayed a course that could easily have imprisoned him in stocks or taken his life. The life he chose laid a foundation for other reformers to follow in his footsteps.

Luther's achievements were an outward expression of an inward conversion that impelled him to follow what he felt was right rather than clinging to the status quo in defending one's rights. The qualities that inspired and motivated him are the same qualities that manifest themselves in a noble and great one.

The 95 Theses was widely circulated throughout Germany and Europe, reaching France, England, and Italy, thus heralding the beginning of the Protestant Reformation.

In 1533, he began serving as the dean of theology at the University of Wittenberg, a post he held until his death.

During his later years, he organized a new church, Lutheranism, and gained many followers. Today, Protestantism is the second-largest faith in Christendom, with 800 to 1 billion followers or 40% of all Christians.

Muhammad The Prophet — born approximately 570 in the Arabian city of Mecca, Muhammad was orphaned at the age of six. According to Islamic doctrine, Muhammad was a prophet sent to preach and confirm the monotheistic teachings of Adam, Abraham, Moses, Jesus, and other prophets. Credited as the founder of Islam, he lived in Mecca from 571 to 632 CE. He is believed to be the author of the most revered book of Islam, the *Koran.*

Muhammad was first raised by a paternal uncle named Abu Talib. In his later years, he would periodically retreat to a mountain cave named Hira for several nights of prayer. When he was 40, Muhammad revealed that the angel Gabriel had visited him in the cave where he received his first revelation from God. In the year 613, Muhammad began preaching these revelations publicly, proclaiming that "God is One" and that complete "submission" (the definition of Islam) to God is the right way of life, aka Din.

Muhammad taught his believers and followers that he was a prophet and messenger of God, similar to the other prophets in Islam. Muhammad is believed to be the final prophet of God in all the main branches of Islam, though some modern denominations diverge from this belief.

In December 629, after many years of fighting with Meccan tribes, Muhammad gathered an army of 10,000 Muslim converts and marched on the city of Mecca. Muhammad seized the city with little bloodshed. In 632, a few months after returning from the Farewell Pilgrimage, he fell ill and died. By the time of his death, most of the Arabian Peninsula had converted to Islam. The revelations (each known as Ayah — literally "Sign [of God]") that Muhammad reported receiving until his death form the verses of the Quran, regarded by Muslims as the verbatim "Word of God" on which the religion is based. Besides the Quran, Muhammad's teachings and practices, found in the Hadith and Sira literature, are also upheld and used as sources of Islamic law.

Pope Francis — born in Buenos Aires, Argentina, in 1936, he became the 266th Pope of the Roman Catholic Church in March 2013. Known the world over for his great humility and approachability, he was the first citizen from the Americas, the first non-European, and the first Jesuit priest to be named Pope.

Before being elected Pope, he served as the Archbishop and Cardinal of Buenos Aires. He was originally christened Jorge Mario Bergoglio.

Throughout his life, Pope Francis continuously and tirelessly worked for the well-being of the poor, which he viewed as his foremost concern. In his own words, "My people are poor and I am one of them."

Unlike his predecessors, Pope Francis chose an informal approach to the Papal office. He declined the usual luxuries offered to a Pope and instead lived a simple and humble lifestyle in the Vatican guesthouse rather than in the papal residence. He also chose to wear a white Cossack instead of a gold one on his first appearance as a pontiff.

Pope Francis strongly supported social outreach, rather than doctrinal battles, to be the church's essential business. His radical thought on humbleness, the practice of simplicity, and austerity towards working out a robust defense of the poor garnered him positive accolades and acclaim.

However, his staunch orthodox discerning against abortion, same-sex marriage, and contraception also drew criticism from the younger generation.

Pope John Paul II — born Karol Jozef Wojtyla in Wadowice, Poland, in 1920, he was the 264th Pope of the Roman Catholic Church. Succeeding Pope John Paul I, he became Pope John Paul II in 1978, the youngest Pope in the history of the Vatican.

John Paul II was the most well-traveled Pontiff of all the Popes. He traveled to 129 countries, including Mexico, Cuba, Ireland, United Kingdom, Egypt, and Israel. His followers would often call him the "Pilgrim Pope" for his extensive travels.

He was instrumental in building relationships between the Catholic church and other faiths around the world. In one of his earliest trips as Pope, he visited Germany in November 1980 and met the leaders of the Lutheran and other Protestant Churches. He also maintained a good relationship with the Church of England. He became the first reigning Pope to travel to the United Kingdom, where he met Queen Elizabeth II, the Supreme Governor of the Church of England.

He is also credited for catalyzing the decline of communism in Central and Eastern Europe. In June 1979, when he visited his homeland of Poland, he was welcomed by an ecstatic crowd. This trip uplifted the spirit of the nation and instigated the Solidarity Movement of 1980.

During his visit to Haiti in March 1983, he bluntly criticized the country's poverty, which inspired massive protests against the ruling government. Soon the dictatorial rule of Jean-Claude "Baby Doc" Duvalier came to an end.

In May 1999, he visited Romania, becoming the first Pope to visit an Eastern Orthodox country since the Great Schism in 1054. In 2001, he traveled to Kazakhstan to celebrate 1700 years of Christianity as the state religion. In

June 2001, he visited Ukraine, an orthodox nation, on the invitation of the President of Ukraine and bishops of the Ukrainian Greek Catholic Church. He also visited Greece in 2001, the first Pope to do so in 1291 years.

He went to great lengths to improve the church's sour relationships with Islam, becoming the first Pope to pray in an Islamic mosque (Umayyad Mosque) in Damascus, Syria, where John the Baptist is believed to have been interred. He even kissed the Holy Quran in Syria, which made him immensely popular with the Muslims though it upset many Catholics.

The relationship between Christianity and Judaism improved during his pontificate, mainly due to his visits to the Auschwitz concentration camp in Poland and the Great Synagogue of Rome. He also set up diplomatic relations with the State of Israel. In April 1994, he hosted The Papal Concert to Commemorate the Holocaust, the first event in the history of the Vatican dedicated to the memories of the six million Jews murdered during World War II.

He maintained a healthy rapport with Buddhists and met with Tenzin Gyatso, the 14th Dalai Lama, eight times.

In May 1981, when he entered the St. Peter's Square to address the audience, he was shot by Mehmet Ali Agca, an expert Turkish gunman belonging to the militant fascist group Grey Wolves. The Pope was seriously injured and underwent a five-hour surgery. A second assassination attempt occurred a year later, in May 1982, when an assailant tried to stab John Paul II with a bayonet in Fatima, Portugal. The assailant was a Spanish priest who claimed that the Pope was an agent of Communist Moscow.

In 2001, he was diagnosed with Parkinson's disease. He also faced difficulties in speaking and hearing and suffered from osteoarthritis. He died in his private apartment on

April 2, 2005, due to heart failure from profound hypotension and circulatory collapse from septic shock.

One of his most important books, *Crossing the Threshold of Hope*, has been published in forty languages and sold millions of copies. His book *Memory and Identity: Conversations at the Dawn of the Millennium* chronicled the rise of evil in Europe, such as Nazism and communism.

He was awarded the Presidential Medal of Freedom, America's highest civilian honor, by President George W. Bush at a ceremony held at the Apostolic Palace in June 2004.

John Paul II was proclaimed venerable on December 19, 2009 by his successor Benedict XVI. He was beatified on May 1, 2011 (Divine Mercy Sunday) after the Congregation for the Causes of Saints attributed one miracle to his intercession, the healing of a French nun called Marie Simon Pierre from Parkinson's disease.

The pontiff's funeral witnessed one of the largest gatherings in history, surpassing the funerals of Winston Churchill and Josip Broz Tito. Four kings, five queens, over 70 presidents and prime ministers, and more than 14 religious leaders attended the funeral. Nearly four million mourners gathered in Rome to show their respect.

Following his death, clergies at the Vatican and around the world started referring to him as "John Paul the Great," making him only the fourth Pope, and the first in the millennium, to receive this honor.

Saint Teresa of Calcutta — more popularly known as Mother Teresa, was born in Skopje, Albania, in 1910. One of the greatest humanitarians of the 20th century, she dedicated her life to serving the poorest of the poor. She founded the Missionaries of Charities in Calcutta, India.

Clad in a white, blue-bordered sari, she and her sisters of the Missionaries of Charity became a symbol of love, care, and compassion for the world. She was a ray of hope for many, including the aged, the destitute, the unemployed, the diseased, the terminally ill, and those abandoned by their families. Blessed with profound empathy, unwavering commitment, and unshakable faith, she turned her back on worldly pleasures and focused on serving humanity.

With her fervent commitment and incredible organizational and managerial skills, she developed the Missionaries of Charity into an international organization that aimed towards helping the impoverished. For her service to humanity, she was honored with the Nobel Peace Prize in 1979. Pope Francis canonized her in September 2016.

Tenzin Gyatso — Dalai Lama is a title given by the Tibetan people for the foremost spiritual leader of the Gelug or "Yellow Hat" school of Tibetan Buddhism, the newest of the classical schools of Tibetan Buddhism.

Dalai Lamas are said to be reincarnated souls in the line of tulkus, who are considered manifestations of the bodhisattva of compassion. Spiritual leaders of Tibetan Buddhism, and in the tradition of Bodhisattva, Dalai Lamas are said to spend their entire life committed to promoting humanity. These souls chose to be reincarnated instead of attaining 'nirvana' to benefit society and mankind. Dalai Lama is a combination of the Mongolian word Dalai and the Tibetan word lama. While the former means ocean, the latter stands for teacher.

The 14th and current Dalai Lama is Tenzin Gyatso, the longest living Dalai Lama in history. He was born in Taktser, Amdo, Tibet, and was selected as the tulku of the

13th Dalai Lama in 1937. Formally recognized as the 14th Dalai Lama at a public declaration in 1939, he assumed full temporal duties in 1950, at the age of 15.

During the 1959 Tibetan uprising, the Dalai Lama fled to India, where he currently lives as a refugee. The 14th Dalai Lama received the Nobel Peace Prize in 1989. *TIME* Magazine named him one of the "Children of Mahatma Gandhi" and his spiritual heir to nonviolence.

He has traveled the world speaking about the welfare of Tibetans, environment, economics, women's rights, non-violence, interfaith dialogue, physics, astronomy, Buddhism and science, cognitive neuroscience, and reproductive health.

The Dalai Lama is an advocate for a world free of nuclear weapons and currently serves on the Nuclear Age Peace Foundation Advisory Council. He voiced his support for the Campaign for the Establishment of a United Nations Parliamentary Assembly, an organization that campaigns for democratic reformation of the United Nations and creating a more accountable international political system.

Giving public talks for non-Buddhist audiences and interviews and teaching Buddhism to large public audiences all over the world, as well as to private groups at his residence in India, appears to be the Dalai Lama's main activity. Despite becoming 80 years old in 2015, he maintains a busy schedule of international lectures and teaching.

His public talks and teachings are usually webcast live in multiple languages, via an inviting organization's website, or on the Dalai Lama's website. Scores of his past teaching videos can be viewed there, as well as public talks, conferences, interviews, dialogues, and panel discussions.

In Dalai Lama's essay, *The Ethic of Compassion*, he expressed his belief that if we only reserve compassion for those whom we love, we are ignoring the responsibility of sharing these characteristics of respect and empathy with those we do not have relationships with, which cannot allow us to "cultivate love." He elaborated upon this idea by writing that, although it takes time to develop a higher level of compassion, eventually we will recognize that empathy will become a part of life and promote our quality as humans and inner strength.

The Dalai Lama sees important common ground between science and Buddhism in having the same approach to challenge dogma based on empirical evidence from observation and analysis of phenomena. Apart from time spent teaching Buddhism and fulfilling his many responsibilities to his Tibetan followers, the Dalai Lama has probably spent, and continues to spend, more of his time and resources investigating the interface between Buddhism and science through the ongoing series of Mind and Life dialogues and its spin-offs than on any other single activity.

In particular, the Mind and Life Education Humanities & Social Sciences initiatives have been instrumental in developing the emerging field of Contemplative Science by researching, for example, the effects of contemplative practice on the human brain, behavior, and biology.

The Dalai Lama is outspoken about environmental problems, frequently giving public talks on themes related to the environment. He was quoted as saying, "Ecology should be part of our daily life." Around 2005, he started campaigning for wildlife conservation, including by issuing a religious ruling against wearing tiger and leopard skins as garments. Before the 2009 United Nations Climate Change Conference, he urged national leaders to put aside domestic concerns and take collective action against climate change.

The Dalai Lama has received numerous awards over his spiritual and political career. In 1959, he received the Ramon Magsaysay Award for Community Leadership. In June 1988, the Dalai Lama was awarded the Dr. Leopold Lucas Prize on behalf of the Protestant faculty of the University of Tübingen by Professor Hans-Jürgen Hermison, who stated that the prize was awarded because of the Dalai Lama's important contribution to the promotion of dialogue between different religions and peoples, as well as to his commitment to tolerance and non-violence.

After the Tiananmen Square protests of 1989, the Norwegian Nobel Committee awarded the Dalai Lama the 1989 Nobel Peace Prize. The Committee officially gave the prize to the Dalai Lama for "the struggle of the liberation of Tibet and the efforts for a peaceful resolution" and "in part a tribute to the memory of Mahatma Gandhi."

In 1994, he received the Freedom Medal from the Roosevelt Institute. In June 2006, he became one of only six people ever to be recognized with Honorary Citizenship by the Governor General of Canada. The Dalai Lama was a 2007 recipient of the Congressional Gold Medal, the highest civilian award bestowed by American lawmakers.

In September 2011, the Dalai Lama issued a statement concerning his reincarnation. He stated, "When I am about ninety, I will consult the high Lamas of the Tibetan Buddhist traditions, the Tibetan public, and other concerned people who follow Tibetan Buddhism, and re-evaluate whether the institution of the Dalai Lama should continue or not. On that basis, we will make a decision. If it is decided that the reincarnation of the Dalai Lama should continue and there is a need for the Fifteenth Dalai Lama to be recognized, responsibility for doing so will primarily rest on the concerned officers of the Dalai Lama's Gaden Phodrang Trust.

They should consult the various heads of the Tibetan Buddhist traditions and the reliable oath-bound Dharma Protectors, who are linked inseparably to the lineage of the Dalai Lamas. They should seek advice and direction from these concerned beings and carry out the procedures of search and recognition in accordance with past tradition. I shall leave clear written instructions about this. Bear in mind that, apart from the reincarnation recognized through such legitimate methods, no recognition or acceptance should be given to a candidate chosen for political ends by anyone, including those in the People's Republic of China."

In an interview with the German newspaper *Welt am Sonntag*, published in September 2014, the Dalai Lama stated, "The institution of the Dalai Lama has served its purpose." He added, "We had a Dalai Lama for almost five centuries. The 14th Dalai Lama now is extremely popular. Let us then finish with a popular Dalai Lama."

Zoroaster, aka Zarathustra — is known as the creator of Zoroastrianism, also known as Mazdayasna. He was born either in Northeast Iran or Southwest Afghanistan into the Spitima clan around the 5th century BC.

Zoroaster was a husband, a father of three sons and three daughters, and a priest within his birth religion. He would become a reformer, advocate, and, to many, a prophet who would challenge the polytheistic religions of his day and establish one of the world's oldest religions. Zoroaster challenged the generally accepted polytheistic religion of the day that included animal sacrifice and the use of intoxicants for ritual purposes. Many of the teachings of Zoroastrians are recorded in the *Gathas*, the core of the *Avesta*, which contains hymns believed to have been written by Zoroaster himself.

Zoroaster rejected the religion of his time with its polytheism and oppressive class structure enforced by the Karvis and Karapans, princes and priests who controlled the ordinary people. Zoroastrians believed in heraldic actions, as evidenced by their symbol of light – the Rooster, which crows a new dawning and fights for good against evil.

According to Zoroastrian belief, Zoroaster began his heralded mission at age 30, as he entered the Daiti river to draw water for a Haoma ceremony. When he emerged, he received a vision of Vohu Manah. After this, Vohu Manah took him to the other six Amesha Spentas, where he received the completion of his vision.

Zoroaster's ideas were not embraced quickly. The local religious authorities opposed his ideas and felt their faith, power, and particularly their rituals, were threatened by Zoroaster's teachings against over-ritual singing religious ceremonies. Many did not like Zoroaster's downgrading of the Daevas to evil spirits.

After 12 years of little success, Zoroaster left his home and traveled to Bactria, where King Vishtaspa and his queen learned of Zoroaster's debating with the religious leaders of the land. The two were so impressed by his efforts they decided to adopt Zoroaster's ideas as the official religion of their kingdom. Zoroaster eventually died in his late 70s.

Zoroastrianism led the pre-Islamic Iranian empires for more than a millennium. Today, it is estimated there are only a little more than 200,000 Zoroastrians around the world, with the majority of Zoroastrians living in India and Iran. The number of worshipers has been declining steadily, though there have been unconfirmed reports of as many as 100,000 converts reported in recent years in Iraqi Kurdistan.

Zoroastrianism is a monotheistic faith based, like most religions, on the influence of good and evil and the belief that good always triumphs in the end. Zoroastrianism teaches of a supreme being named Ahura Mazda (Wise Lord) and includes messianism, good works, a final judgment, and heaven and hell. It is plausible this early religion laid a foundation and springboard for future spiritual leaders and religions such as Judaism, Gnosticism, Christianity, Islam, and Buddhism.

The most important texts within the Zoroastrianism religion are those of the *Avesta*, which includes Zoroaster's writings referred to as the *Gathas*. These enigmatic poems define the religion's precepts and purpose. Zoroaster proclaimed monotheism and that the God of Heaven was the sustaining force of the Universe. He believed in the God-given right of agency and the consequences of the choices we make.

Zoroastrians profess the purpose in life is to "be among those who renew the world...to make the world progress towards perfection." Its tenants include there is only one path, "The path of Truth." Choose the right thing because it is the right thing to do, and all good things will come your way. Good deeds lead to happiness and keep chaos at bay. These are tenants of nobility that lead to great accomplishments.

CHAPTER 7

The Intellectual Rulers

The brain is the most complex part of the human body. It is the central nervous system and control center for all cognitive and non-cognitive thought. The field of mental capacity is broad and difficult to measure.

We often describe the mentally gifted with exciting adjectives such as brilliant, genius, mental giant, brainiac, or someone who "blows the bell curve." These highly intelligent people possess a seemingly gifted and unique way of processing the data they ingest that allows them to see new applications for objects, circumstances, or situations that you or I might overlook.

Although there are many facets of the mentally gifted, one standard has been almost universally accepted throughout recent history as the primary method of identifying the intellectually endowed. That method can be summed up in just two letters, I.Q. The IQ (Intelligence Quotient) test identifies and quantifies mental giftedness as those who are academically placed in the top two percent of the population, maintaining an average IQ of 130 or above. Throughout history, and in the present day, there have been many individuals who have blown the bell curve when it came to IQ scores. We will highlight several of them as we proceed further in this chapter.

About IQ

The abbreviation "IQ" comes from the term intelligence quotient. It was first coined in 1912, by William Stern, a Jew who emigrated to the United States after being ousted by Hitler's regime following the rise of Nazi power. Stern, a leading youth psychologist and one of the foremost authorities in differential psychology, introduced the concept of intelligence testing, or the intelligence quotient. The testing method consists of dividing the developmental age by the chronological age. Stern spent his final years of life as a professor at Duke University. He died in 1938.

To date, only a handful of public schools have added provisions for identifying and implementing procedures that support mentally gifted children. Our society could garner numerous benefits if our educational system implemented programs that provide a more independent and conducive environment for mentally gifted children. These children require a unique environment to accelerate their advancement.

While IQ is a numerical method for measuring intelligence within a person, other determinates can also indicate intellectual dominance. These include mastering a language, artistic and musical proficiency, social/emotional skills, and spiritual abilities that could also be considered giftedness.

Between the 1980s and 1990s, research conducted by Raymond Cattell, J. P. Guilford, and Louis Thurstone provided data supporting the premise that there are multiple components of intelligence, including motivation, high self-concept, and creativity as examples of giftedness.

In 1978, Joseph Renzulli introduced his "three-ring" definition of giftedness, proposing that behavioral habits shape giftedness rather than genetics. Renzulli taught gifted behavior could be measured by three basic human traits: ability, task commitment, and high creativity.

The U.S. Federal Government threw its hat into the ring by publishing a statutory definition of "gifted and talented." The statute states, "The term 'gifted and talented' when used in respect to students, children, or youth means students, children, or youth who give evidence of high-performance capability in areas such as intellectual, creative, artistic, or leadership capacity, or in specific academic fields, and who require services or activities not ordinarily provided by the school to fully develop such capabilities."

Gifted children sometimes develop asynchronously, a condition in which their minds are ahead of their physical growth. Certain cognitive and emotional functions develop differently and in non-congruent stages of development. Several post-Freudian experts believe gifted children may advance more quickly through stages. Because these gifted individuals experience the world differently, they often act uniquely on social and emotional issues.

Francoys Gagne's Differentiated Model of Giftedness and Talent (DMGT) is a developmental theory that distinguishes giftedness from talent, explaining how outstanding natural abilities (gifts) develop into specific expert skills (talents). Per the DMGT theory, "one cannot become talented without first being gifted, or almost so." The model is based on six components that can interact in countless and unique ways that foster moving from natural abilities (giftedness) to systematically developed skills.

It is generally agreed that gifted children differ from their peers in ways other than intellectual ability alone. Evidence of this was found in 1921 by the American psychologist Lewis M. Terman, who initiated a study of more than 1,500 gifted children with IQs higher than 140. The results of the study determined that as high IQ children aged, their drive and desire to achieve, along with greater mental and social adjustment, increased among the gifted group compared with non-gifted children.

In another early 20th-century study, which focused on children with IQs greater than 180, psychologist Leta Hollingworth found that individuals within this group were overly sensitive to how they differed from others and often suffered from problems such as boredom and rejection by their peers.

In theory, there are three ways of educating children who are intellectually and academically more advanced than their peers: (1) acceleration, whereby the gifted child is allowed to learn material at a more rapid pace or is promoted more rapidly through grades; (2) enrichment, whereby the gifted child works through the usual grades at the usual pace, but with a curriculum supplemented by a variety of cultural activities; and (3) differentiation, whereby gifted children are accelerated or enriched within the regular classroom.

There are plenty of intelligent people in the world, yet just a handful are recognized as intellectual geniuses. Many of us are prone to judge intelligence by material achievement rather than one's ability to use reason or problem-solving skills. Some individuals possess a higher level of mental strength than others. These individuals can endure tremendous emotional and physical adversity with a quiet dignity that may emotionally unravel others.

Whether found in the two highest percentiles of the Intelligence Quotient, music virtuosos, or the most gifted athletes in the world, few can argue that gifted individuals draw our wonderment, admiration, and awe. Unfortunately, in some instances, they can also receive our judgment and disapproval.

The following individuals have historically exhibited qualities of mental greatness. Unarguably, many others could be added to the list of mental giftedness, yet may not have received formal or public recognition. Nevertheless, their accomplishments are worth recognizing.

Leonardo Da Vinci was born in 1452. His family was poor but provided the basic needs that allowed him to pursue his passion for painting.

Qualifying as a master artist at age 20, he spent his entire life perfecting his painting, pastel drawing, sculpting, carpentry, and metalworking skills.

His notebooks contain thousands of sketches, personal notes, and discoveries that reflect his brilliance for invention and his thorough understanding of natural science and human anatomy. Some of these drawings include images of complex machinery, flying inventions, and bicycles. He also drew sketches of intricate anatomical drawings of human organs and skeletal bones.

A man a century ahead of his time, he was the first person to research the mechanics of human anatomy. Our understanding of his brilliance took hundreds of years to determine and was only discovered when we had the necessary technology to measure and understand his findings. Da Vinci theorized geographic time while all others were still wondering about the size, shape, and volume of the earth.

Da Vinci was not only an astronomer; he was also a genius in science, engineering, and art. It is remarkable to consider the many mysteries of science he uncovered with almost no technological expertise or schooling. His indomitable curiosity for anything and everything made him an unparalleled inventor, a talented artist, and a remarkable engineer. While many accomplishments of geniuses are often one dimensional, Da Vinci appears to have had multidimensional ability in almost every direction he chose to follow.

Isaac Newton was a great visualizer and a broad thinker. He hit his head with an apple, and he became one of the smartest men known in history. He single-handedly invented calculus, one of the most important mathematics tools, and composed a model of the universe that we still use today to make predictions about how things should work.

Newton expanded human knowledge substantially. He laid a foundation for other geniuses such as Planck, Einstein, and Bohr to build upon. It is amazing to consider how much he accomplished in the first quarter-century of his life. Newton's name extended beyond that of other scientists. He was regarded as "the world's first scientific genius." Newton was a national hero, though his influence extended far beyond Britain.

Stephen Hawking was born in Oxford, England, into a family of doctors on January 8, 1942. Hawking began his university education at University College, Oxford, in October 1959 at age 17, where he received a first-class BA degree in physics. He began his graduate work at Trinity Hall, Cambridge, in October 1962, where he attained his Ph.D. degree in applied mathematics and theoretical physics, specializing in general relativity and cosmology in March 1966.

In 1974, Hawking sent shock waves throughout the physics world with his achievement that black holes radiate. The result provided mankind's first glimpse of uniting quantum theory with general relativity, which before this time seemed irreconcilable. It also set the direction for theoretical physics.

Hawking was the first person to lay out a theory of cosmology explained by a union of the theories of relativity and quantum mechanics. He was a vigorous supporter of the many-worlds interpretation of quantum mechanics.

His book, *A Brief History of Time,* appeared on the *Sunday Times* bestseller list for a record-breaking 237 weeks. Hawking was a Fellow of the Royal Society and a lifetime member of the Pontifical Academy of Sciences. He received the Presidential Medal of Freedom, the highest civilian award in the United States. In 2002, Hawking was ranked number 25 in the BBC's poll of the 100 Greatest Britons.

In 1963, at 21 years of age, Hawking was diagnosed with Amyotrophic Lateral Sclerosis, aka ALS, one of the most destructive neurodegenerative diseases impacting its host. Insidiously, relentlessly, and in most cases expeditiously, the disease makes its inroads paralyzing its victim, causing respiratory failure and death within four to five years. Miraculously, Hawking survived the disease for 55 years. He died in 2018 at the age of 76, making him the longest known survivor of the disease.

Galileo Galilei, aka the Polymath from Pisa, was a genius in astronomy.

Among his other nicknames, Galileo was known as the "father of observational astronomy," the "father of modern physics," the "father of the scientific method," and the "father of modern science."

Galileo studied a range of subjects, including speed, velocity, inertia, gravity and free fall, the principle of relativity, and projectile motion. Additionally, he invented the thermoscope and various military compasses and used the telescope for scientific observations of celestial objects. His observations include the telescopic confirmation of the phases of Venus, the observation of the four largest satellites (or moons) of Jupiter, the observation of Saturn's rings, and the analysis of sunspots.

His championing of heliocentrism garnered criticism from within the Catholic Church and opponents in the astronomy community. The Roman Inquisition, which investigated the matter in 1615, concluded that "heliocentrism was foolish and absurd in philosophy and formally heretical since it explicitly contradicts in many places the sense of Holy Scripture."

Galileo later defended his views in *Dialogue Concerning the Two Chief World Systems* (1632), which appeared to attack Pope Urban VIII and thus alienated both the Pope and the Jesuits, who had supported Galileo until this point. He was tried by the Inquisition, found "vehemently suspect of heresy," and forced to recant.

He spent the rest of his life under house arrest. During this time, he wrote *Two New Sciences* (1638), primarily concerning kinematics and the strength of materials, summarizing work he had done some forty years earlier.

Although Galileo was not the sole inventor of the telescope, it could be argued that he was the final contributor and driving force to bring it to market. He spent much of his life promoting it and seeking to earn a living through selling them. It could be said, "The telescope led him to the stars, that led him to the universe, that led him to science."

Charles Darwin was an intelligently insightful man whose creativity and imagination allowed him to see things that others could not. His theory of evolution by natural selection, first formulated in Darwin's book *On the Origin of Species* in 1859, is the process by which organisms change over time as a result of changes in heritable physical or behavioral traits. Changes that allow an organism to better adapt to its environment will help it survive and have more offspring.

Evolution by natural selection is one of the best substantiated theories in the history of science, supported by evidence from a wide variety of scientific disciplines, including paleontology, geology, genetics, and developmental biology. There are also social applications to the theory that can influence social prowess, dating, and marital success.

"The theory has two main points," said Brian Richmond, curator of human origins at the American Museum of Natural History in New York City. "All life on Earth is connected and related to each other," and this diversity of life is a product of "modifications of populations by natural selection, where some traits were favored in an environment over others," he said.

More simply put, the theory can be described as "descent with modification," said Briana Pobiner, an anthropologist and educator at the Smithsonian Institution National Museum of Natural History in Washington, D.C., who specializes in the study of human origins. Darwin's theory is sometimes described as "survival of the fittest," but that can be misleading, Pobiner said. Here, "fitness" refers not to an organism's strength or athletic ability, but rather the ability to survive and reproduce.

For example, his ideas of animals adapting their survival instincts to their surroundings and the impact of food supply changes giving animals with more suitable traits an advantage to survive and rear similar offspring, thereby changing animal characteristics over time, was brilliant.

A study on human evolution on 1,900 students, published online in the journal *Personality and Individual Differences* in October 2017, found that many people may have trouble finding a mate because of rapidly changing social and technological advances that are evolving faster than humans. "Nearly one in two individuals faces considerable difficulties in the domain of mating," said lead study author Menelaos Apostolou, an associate professor of social sciences at the University of Nicosia in Cyprus. "In most cases, these difficulties are not due to something wrong or broken, but due to people living in an environment which is very different from the environment they evolved to function in."

This begs the question, "Is your evolutionary path adversely impacting your social path? What role has nature and nurture played in your dating outcomes? If you can identify, isolate, and eliminate the issue, would the odds of finding and pairing with a suitable partner increase?

It can take nobility, meekness, and a willing dose of humility to find answers to these difficult questions. Patience and PR (Personal Revelation) cannot be overstated as well.

Benjamin Franklin was a genius in science, literature, politics, people skills, and inventions. In addition, he was an exceptional leader. People of the time looked to Franklin as the authority in each of the life categories he excelled in. His strong moral principles compelled him to engage in issues he deemed as important.

For example, he changed the world to a large degree when he abandoned his British loyalties and aligned his actions and support with the new Colonial Patriots.

The deciding factor was the British stance on taxation without representation. Franklin recognized the agenda as an act of pride, dominance, and tyranny, rather than a respect for freedom and justice. Per Franklin's view, the British monarchy sought to enforce their perceived rights rather than simply doing what was right.

Franklin was a true patriot and one of America's first ambassadors. His efforts contributed to the establishment of the United States of America as a free democracy. Had he and other great patriots lacked the courage to act fervently, morally, and expeditiously, the U.S as we now know it would be quite different than it is today. In later life, Franklin campaigned to abolish slavery.

Franklin was a champion for developing institutions that would improve society. He co-founded America's first circulating library, known as the Library Company of Philadelphia. He founded America's first volunteer fire department, the Union Fire Co. He established America's first learned society, called the American Philosophical Society; America's first liberal arts academy, Pennsylvania Academy & College, now the University of Pennsylvania; America's first public hospital, Pennsylvania Hospital; and America's first mutual insurance company, The Philadelphia Contribution ship. He also proposed the concept of Daylight Savings Time.

Thomas Alva Edison, born in 1847, was an American and businessman who earned the distinction of being referred to as America's greatest inventor. Edison's passions, as with his predecessor Franklin, extended much further than just electricity.

Edison envisioned far more applications for electricity than simply lighting a darkened room or corridor. He used it to power his many inventions, including electric power generation, mass communication, sound recording, and motion pictures. These inventions, which include the phonograph, the motion picture camera, and the long-lasting, practical electric light bulb, had a widespread impact on the modern industrialized world.

He was one of the first inventors to apply mass production and teamwork principles to the invention process, working with many researchers and employees. He is often credited with establishing the first industrial research laboratory. He was a prolific inventor, holding 1,093 US patents in his name.

Early in his career, Edison worked as a telegraph operator, which inspired some of his earliest inventions. In 1876, he established his first laboratory facility in Menlo Park, New Jersey, where many of his early inventions would be developed. He would later establish a botanic laboratory in Fort Myers, Florida, in collaboration with businessmen Henry Ford and Harvey Firestone, and a laboratory in West Orange, New Jersey, that featured the world's first film studio, the Black Maria.

Albert Einstein was the greatest theoretical scientist the world has ever known and the father of what has become known as the two pillars of modern physics, the theory of relativity and quantum physics.

Einstein's communication skills were almost non-existent until he was four years of age. Fortunately, his fluency and accomplishments in later years more than made up for any childhood deficiency. Psychologist and cognitive scientist Steven Pinker, an expert in cognitive thought, has suggested that rather than viewing Einstein's early development skills as a disorder and his later genius, they may each have been developmentally intrinsic to one another.

Einstein was a voracious learner. He connected with theoretical revolutionary icons such as Galileo and Isaac Newton, whose thoughts inspired his own. He was also influenced by the life and accomplishments of Mahatma Gandhi. In college, he became interested in electromagnetism, but found the curriculum lacking. Encouraged by a classmate to further research the subject independently, Einstein authored his theory of electronegativity.

Einstein's theory of relativity ($E=mc^2$) became the formula upon which nuclear energy is created. His findings in the field of gravity have made a significant contribution to space travel and design.

Upon realizing the devastating potential of the atomic bomb being created by other German scientists, Einstein wrote a detailed personal letter to President Franklin Roosevelt urging that preventative defensive measures be taken. Unfortunately, the result was the bombings of Hiroshima and Nagasaki in Japan.

A few of Einstein's most notable quotes include:

Two things are infinite: the universe and human stupidity; and I am not sure about the universe.

Science without religion is lame; religion without science is blind.

The most beautiful thing we can experience is the mysterious; it is the source of all true art and science.

Einstein played an important role in creating awareness of Attention Deficit Hyperactivity Disorder (ADHD), an infliction from which he suffered. The condition is a metabolic disorder in the brain triggered by genetic factors and includes significant anomalies in the brain's neurotransmitter system. These anomalies are triggered by an imbalance of the neurotransmitters dopamine and noradrenaline, which play an important role in transmitting stimuli in nerve cells. When these neurotransmitters are out of balance, faulty information processing will result in the affected areas of the brain.

Several psychosocial factors may encourage the development of the disorder, such as an unstructured daily routine, unreliable living conditions, premature birth, alcohol, nicotine, or drug consumption during pregnancy, and lack of exercise.

Nikola Tesla is an under-rated and somewhat forgotten genius. Born in Smiljan, Croatia, in 1856, he lived to the age of 87. Tesla had few mentors and a smaller base of knowledge that preceded him.

His intellectual genius surfaced early. His ability to complete integral calculus in his head and recite entire books from memory were just two examples of his remarkable intellect. Photographic memory and a gift for visualization were two added qualities that placed him well ahead of the intellectuals of his day.

Tesla blew the bell curve in his development of new processes and inventions. His mind never rested as he continually focused his thoughts on new discoveries. While others may have focused on a single discovery, his mind was always as if it was at a clearing where all things were possible. His contributions in AC electricity changed the world as we know it today.

He is remembered most for inventing the induction motor, an AC electric motor that uses electric current to produce torque through electromagnetic induction. This motor is the foundation for electric vehicles. Tesla also pioneered other discoveries that were equally prolific. His passion and intellect extended much further than just motors.

Here are a few of the other projects he worked to develop and produce:

- Wireless transmission of electricity transmitted from power stations to vehicles and homes by a receiving antenna.

- An electric submarine.

- Teleforce, a defensive weapon that fired pellets from a vacuum chamber via electrostatic repulsion.

- The Death Ray, only to be used when unavoidable.

- The Mechanical Oscillator, to produce liquid-free air through compression.

- Renewable electricity and heat through natural energy sources.

- An Earthquake Machine, a device small enough to fit in your pocket, yet powerful enough to level a house.

- A Force Field large enough to protect a city from attack during wars.

- A Flying Machine, shaped like a cigar or saucer and fueled electro-mechanically.

- Thought Camera, a device that would have the capability to photograph thoughts, based on his theory that a definite image in thought must produce a corresponding image on the eye's retina.

Historical data suggests Tesla's lifetime work may account for an astounding 700 patents, although less than half of them are truly substantiated. Tesla was one of the greatest geniuses the world has under appreciated.

William James Sidis was an American child prodigy with exceptional mathematical and linguistic skills. Sidis is notable for his 1920 book *The Animate and the Inanimate*, in which he postulates the existence of dark matter, entropy, and the origin of life in the context of thermodynamics.

Sidis's parents believed in nurturing a precocious and fearless love of knowledge (but their parenting methods were criticized in the media and retrospectively). Sidis could read *The New York Times* at 18 months. By age eight, he had reportedly taught himself eight languages, Latin, Greek, French, Russian, German, Hebrew, Turkish, and Armenian. He even created his own language he called "Vendergood."

Although Harvard University had previously refused to let his father enroll him at age nine because he was still a child, Sidis set a record in 1909 by becoming the youngest person to enroll at the school.

Sidis first became famous for his precocity, then later for his eccentricity and withdrawal from public life. Eventually, he avoided mathematics altogether, writing on other subjects under several pseudonyms. He claimed to have an extremely high IQ and to be conversant in about 25 languages and dialects. Some of these claims have not been verifiable, but peers such as Norbert Wiener supported the assertion that his intelligence was extremely high.

In early 1910, Sidis's mastery of higher mathematics was such that he lectured the Harvard Mathematical Club on four-dimensional bodies.

In *The Animate and the Inanimate*, Sidis predicted the existence of regions of space where the second law of thermodynamics operated in reverse to the temporal direction we experience. Everything outside of what we would today call a galaxy would be such a region. Sidis claimed that the matter in this region would not generate light.

Sidis was outspoken about his pacifism. In 1919, Sidis was arrested for participating in a socialist May Day parade in Boston that turned violent. He was sentenced to 18 months in prison under the Sedition Act of 1918. During the trial, Sidis stated that he had been a conscientious objector to the World War I draft, was a socialist, and did not believe in a god like the "big boss of the Christians," but rather in something that is in a way apart from a human being. He later developed his libertarian philosophy based on individual rights and "the American social continuity."

Current Day Mentally Gifted Ones

Garry Kasparov, who has an IQ of 190, shocked the world in 2003 when he reached a draw against a chess computer with the ability to calculate three million positions per second. He became the world champion chess player and grandmaster of chess at age 22 when he defeated Anatoly Karpov.

Kasparov made his Olympiad debut in 1980. At just 17 years of age, he became the youngest player to represent the Soviet Union. He competed in eight Olympiads and took home a gold medal from each of them. Kasparov holds the record for most consecutive professional tournament victories, placing first or equal first in 15 individual tournaments from 1981 to 1990.

Philip Emeagwali has an IQ of 190. A Nigerian-born engineer, mathematician, computer scientist, geologist, and Nobel Prize recipient, he developed a way to use a supercomputer to detect undiscovered petroleum fields. His contribution is significant as there are still many fossil fuels needed in many underdeveloped parts of the world

Marilyn vos Savant is listed in the Guinness Book of World Records as one of the world's smartest women, with an IQ score measured as high as 228. She is a popular columnist for *Parade Magazine*. Her readers "Ask Marilyn" how to solve puzzles and pose questions on different subjects.

Mislav Predavec a, Croatian math professor, is ranked 7th on the list of the ten most intelligent people in the world. He is the founder and president of the GenerIQ Society, an elite organization with many of the world's most intelligent people. His IQ has been measured at 192.

At first glance, you might think Rick Rosner is an average Joe. After all, he is rough and tough and was a bar bouncer for several years. But you would be wrong. He has an IQ of 192 and is a former television producer. In the late 70s, he created the TV series *CHIPS*, and later in his career he developed a portable satellite television in partnership with DirecTV.

Christopher Langan is an American autodidact (self-taught) with an IQ reportedly between 195 and 210. Langan has been described as "the smartest man in America" and "the smartest man in the world" by various media sources. Talking at six months and reading at age three, Langan developed a "theory of the relationship between mind and reality" that he labeled the Cognitive Theoretic Model of the Universe (CTMU).

Dr. Evangelos Katsioulis is a Greek national medical doctor and psychiatrist. His academic accomplishments include degrees in philosophy, medical research technology, and psychopharmacology. Katsioulis is the founder of two intelligence-related organizations, the World Intelligence Network (WIN), an international organization of high IQ societies, and AAAA.GR, a pioneer voluntary team for the detection and support of gifted individuals in Greece. His IQ has been measured at 198.

Kim Ung-Yong has a verified IQ of 210. A Korean civil engineer, Kim is considered a master child prodigy. At the age of 6 months, he could speak and understand Korean and other languages. At the age of 3 years, he could read in several languages, including Korean, Japanese, German, and English. He was listed in the *Guinness Book of World Records* under Highest IQ and was known for solving complex calculus problems on live television.

Christopher Hirata has a verified IQ of 225. When just 13, he made waves by getting a gold medal at the International Physics Olympiad. At 16, he was working with NASA in its mission of conquering Mars. He obtained his Ph.D. at Princeton University at the age of 22. A bonified child genius, Hirata is currently teaching astrophysics at the California Institute of Technology.

Terrence Tao has a verified IQ of 230. Tao is an Australian-born Chinese American mathematician working in harmonic analysis, partial differential equations, additive combinatorics, ergodic Ramsey theory, random matrix theory, and analytic number theory. Another child prodigy, this genius taught arithmetic to a five-year-old when he was all of two years old. At just eight years of age, Tao achieved a score of 760 on the pre-1995 SAT. He attended mathematics courses at the university level when he was just nine years old.

At 14, Tao attended the Research Science Institute. At 16, he received both his Bachelor's and Master's degrees and by 20 received his Ph.D. from Princeton. At age 24, he became the youngest full professor to teach at UCLA. Tao remains the youngest winner to date of all the three medals in Olympiads. He received the 2003 Clay Research Award, the Bôcher Memorial Prize in 2002, and the Salem Prize in 2000.

Sir Timothy John Berners-Lee is an English engineer and computer scientist, most known as the World Wide Web inventor. Berners-Lee's parents introduced their son to computer science by their contributions to the first commercially built computer, the Ferranti Mark I. Berners-Lee was a keen trainspotter as a child and his interest in electronics began by tinkering with a model railway.

He studied at The Queen's College, Oxford, from 1973 to 1976, where he received a first-class bachelor of arts degree in physics. While he was at university, Berners-Lee made a computer out of an old television set he bought from a repair shop.

In 1989, he proposed an information management system (IMS) and implemented the first successful communication between a Hypertext Transfer Protocol (HTTP) client and server via the Internet. The first website was built at CERN. The website was put online on August 6, 1991 with info.cern.ch as the address of the world's first website and web server, running on a NeXT computer at CERN. The first webpage address was:

http://info.cern.ch/hypertext/WWW/TheProject.html

It centered on information regarding the World Wide Web project.

Berners-Lee is one of the pioneer voices in favor of net neutrality. He has strongly expressed the view that Internet Service Providers (ISPs) should supply "connectivity with no strings attached." He also advocates that ISPs should neither control nor monitor the browsing activities of customers without their expressed consent. He supports the idea that net neutrality is a kind of human social network right. "Threats to the internet, such as companies or governments that interfere with or snoop on internet traffic, compromise basic human network rights," says Berners-Lee.

In 1994, Berners-Lee founded the World Wide Web Consortium (W3C) at the Massachusetts Institute of Technology. It comprised various companies that were willing to create standards and recommendations to improve the Web's quality. Berners-Lee made his idea available freely, with no patent and no royalties due. W3C decided that its standards should be based on royalty-free technology, so anyone could easily adopt them.

He is the founder of the World Wide Web Foundation and is a senior researcher and holder of the 3Com founder's chair at the MIT Computer Science and Artificial Intelligence Laboratory (CSAIL). Berners-Lee is also a director of the Web Science Research Initiative (WSRI) and the MIT Center for Collective Intelligence advisory board. In 2011, he was named as a member of the board of trustees for the Ford Foundation. He is a co-founder and president of the Open Data Institute and an advisor at Memes, a social media network site that can create GIF images and operates as a medium for the "cultural transmission" of ideas in general, where customs and ideas spread from brain to brain.

Queen Elizabeth II knighted Berners-Lee for his services to the global development of the Internet. He received the Turing award, aka "The Nobel Prize of Computing," in 2016 for inventing the World Wide Web, the first web browser, and the fundamental protocols and algorithms allowing the Web to scale.

Named in *TIME* Magazine's list of the 100 Most Important People of the 20th century, Berners-Lee has received many other accolades for his inventions. He was honored as the "Inventor of the World Wide Web" during the 2012 Summer Olympics opening ceremony. He appeared in person working with a vintage NeXT Computer at the London Olympic Stadium. He tweeted, "This is for everyone," which was instantly spelled out in LCD lights attached to the chairs of the 80,000 people in the audience.

In September 2018, Berners-Lee announced a new application made by open-source startup Irrupt, based on the Solid standards. This application aims to give users more control over their personal data, allowing them to choose where the data goes, who is allowed to see certain elements, and which apps are allowed to see that data.

CHAPTER 8

The Exploring Rulers

In the original television series *Star Trek*, William Shatner, as Captain Kirk Commander of the USS Enterprise, along with his First Assistant Mr. Spock from the planet Vulcan, journeyed into the unknown regions of the universe to seek out new life forms and civilizations and "boldly go where no man has gone before."

It is unlikely that the series screenwriter, producer, and creator Eugene Wesley Roddenberry had any idea of the popularity, momentum, and staying power his series would have on its viewers and future "Trekkies." The draw of the *Star Trek* series, which began in 1966 and lasted three seasons, continues today and shows no signs of ending any time soon. Trek craze has grown through the production and distribution of 13 phenomenally successful motion pictures.

The allure of being the first person to discover a new continent, a new civilization, and new resources that can support future habitation, expansion, and possibilities, has impelled monarchies, philanthropists, and benefactors to embark upon discovery expeditions since the dawn of mankind. The visionaries, advocates, and emissaries who are the driving forces for new discoveries are referred to as explorers.

The following explorers were chosen by the magnitude of their accomplishments and their impact on humanity.

Neil Alden Armstrong was an American astronaut and aeronautical engineer who was the first person to walk on the Moon. He was also a naval aviator, test pilot, and university professor. He made his first spaceflight as the command pilot of Gemini 8 in March 1966, becoming NASA's first civilian astronaut to fly in space. During this mission with pilot David Scott, he performed the first docking of two spacecraft. The mission was aborted early after Armstrong used some of his reentry control fuel to stabilize a dangerous roll caused by a stuck thruster.

During training for Armstrong's second and last spaceflight, as commander of Apollo 11, he had to eject from the Lunar Landing Research Vehicle moments before a crash. On July 20, 1969, Armstrong and Apollo 11 Lunar Module (LM) pilot Buzz Aldrin became the first people to land on the Moon. The next day they spent two and a half hours outside the Lunar Module *Eagle* spacecraft while Michael Collins remained in lunar orbit in the Apollo Command Module *Columbia*. When Armstrong stepped onto the lunar surface, he famously said: "That's one small step for [a] man, one giant leap for mankind."

Along with Collins and Aldrin, Armstrong was awarded the Presidential Medal of Freedom by President Richard Nixon. President Jimmy Carter presented Armstrong with the Congressional Space Medal of Honor in 1978, and Armstrong and his former crewmates received a Congressional Gold Medal in 2009.

Christopher Columbus was an Italian explorer and navigator who completed four voyages from Spain across the Atlantic Ocean, opening the way for European exploration and colonization of the Americas. He led three Spanish galleons, the *Niña*, *Pinta*, and *Santa Maria*, during his first voyage. His expeditions, sponsored by the Catholic Monarchs of Spain, are commonly accepted to be the first European contact with the Caribbean, Central America, and South America.

Columbus's expeditions inaugurated a period of exploration, conquest, and colonization that lasted for centuries, helping create the modern Western world. The transfers between the Old World and New World that followed his first voyage are known as the Columbian exchange. Many landmarks and institutions in the Western Hemisphere bear his name, including the country of Colombia and the District of Columbia.

Marco Polo is forever linked to the world of exploration. In the book *The Travels of Marco Polo*, this famed explorer's adventures and journeys are detailed as he explored the continent of Asia and met Kublai Khan.

Polo was born in 1254, in Venice, Italy. Although he was born to a wealthy Venetian merchant family, much of Polo's childhood was parentless, as an extended family raised him. Polo's mother died when he was young, and his father and uncle, Niccolo and Maffeo Polo, successful jewel merchants, spent their time in Asia for much of Polo's youth.

Niccolo and Maffeo's journeys brought them into present-day China. They joined a diplomatic mission to the court of Kublai Khan, the Mongol leader whose grandfather, Genghis Khan, had conquered Northeast Asia. In 1269, the two men returned to Venice and immediately started making plans for their return to Khan's court. During their stay with the leader, Khan had expressed his interest in Christianity and asked the Polo brothers to visit again with 100 priests and a collection of holy water.

Khan's Empire, the largest the world had ever seen, was largely a mystery to those living within the Holy Roman Empire's borders. A sophisticated culture outside the reaches of the Vatican seemed unfathomable, yet that is exactly what the Polo brothers described to confounded Venetians when they arrived home.

Kublai Khan eventually employed Polo as a special envoy to far-flung areas of Asia never before explored by Europeans, including Burma, India, and Tibet. With Polo, as always, was a stamped metal packet from Khan himself that served as his official credentials from the powerful leader.

Ferdinand Magellan was the first sailor to circumnavigate the seas from the Atlantic Ocean and cross the Pacific Ocean. He discovered the Philippines, where we was killed in the Battle of Mactan. After King Manuel I of Portugal refused to support his plan to reach India by a new route, by sailing around the southern end of the South American continent, he was eventually selected by King Charles I of Spain to search for a westward route to the Maluku Islands (the "Spice Islands"). Commanding a fleet of five vessels, he headed south through the Atlantic Ocean to Patagonia. Despite a series of storms and mutinies, they made it through the Strait of Magellan into a body of water he named the "peaceful sea" (the modern Pacific Ocean).

His name is associated not only with things explored during his voyages but also with the stars and galaxies above us. A Portuguese explorer, Magellan organized the Spanish expedition to the East Indies from 1519 to 1522, resulting in the first circumnavigation of the Earth, which was completed by Juan Sebastián Elcano.

Spanish conquistador Hernan Cortés conquered and colonized parts of South America. Cortés was successful in reaching Mayan territory along the Yucatan Peninsula, leading to his conquest of Mexico. Most notably, he is known for his overthrow of the Aztec empire. It should be noted that Cortés used his own money for the expeditions he undertook, leaving him heavily in debt. Cortés was part of a generation of Spanish explorers and conquistadors who began the first phase of the Spanish colonization of the Americas. Today's understanding of the personality and motivation has done little to enlarge understanding regarding him. As a result of historical trends, descriptions of Cortés tend to be demeaning or idealizing.

Second Lieutenant William Clark and Captain Meriwether Lewis led the Corps of Discovery Expedition of the western United States in 1804. This took place just after the US completed the Louisiana Purchase. They explored the western United States beginning in Missouri through to the Pacific coast.

President Thomas Jefferson commissioned the expedition shortly after the Louisiana Purchase in 1803 to explore and to map the newly acquired territory, to find a practical route across the western half of the continent, and to establish an American presence in this territory before Britain and other European powers tried to claim it. The campaign's secondary objectives were scientific and economic: to study the area's plants, animal life, and geography, and to establish trade with local American Indian tribes. The expedition returned to St. Louis to report its findings to Jefferson, with maps, sketches, and journals in hand.

Native American Sacagawea came from the Lemhi Shoshone tribe and was just 16 years of age when she became a guide and interpreter for the exploration of Lewis and Clark. She joined the expedition from North Dakota and helped lead the expedition to the Pacific Ocean. Sacagawea was credited with establishing critical cultural contacts with Native American populations during the two-year journey and contributing to the natural history of the United States.

The National American Woman Suffrage Association of the early 20th century adopted her as a symbol of women's worth and independence, erecting several statues and plaques in her memory and doing much to spread the story of her accomplishments. While the spelling and pronunciation of her name have varied over the years, one thing is certain — her role in the exploration of the western United States cannot be underestimated.

James Cook was born in Marton, Yorkshire, England. He was an explorer, navigator, cartographer, and captain in the British Royal Navy. After making detailed maps of Newfoundland, he led three voyages to the Pacific Ocean. He achieved the first recorded European contact with the eastern coastline of Australia and the Hawaiian Islands and the first recorded circumnavigation of New Zealand.

Cook joined the British merchant navy as a teenager and joined the Royal Navy in 1755. He saw action in the Seven Years War and subsequently surveyed and mapped much of the entrance to the Saint Lawrence River during the siege of Quebec, which brought him to the attention of the Admiralty and the Royal Society. This acclaim came at a crucial moment in his career and the direction of British overseas exploration at the time. It also led to his commission in 1766 as commander of the *HMS Endeavour* for the first of three Pacific voyages.

In these voyages, Cook sailed thousands of miles across largely uncharted areas of the globe. He mapped lands from New Zealand to Hawaii in the Pacific Ocean in greater detail and on a scale not previously charted by Western explorers. He surveyed and named features and recorded islands and coastlines on European maps for the first time. He displayed a combination of seamanship, superior surveying, cartographic skills, physical courage, and an ability to lead men in adverse conditions.

Cook was attacked and killed in 1779 during his third exploratory voyage in the Pacific while attempting to kidnap the Island of Hawaii's monarch, Kalani'ōpu'u, in order to reclaim a cutter stolen from one of his ships. He left a legacy of scientific and geographical knowledge that influenced his successors well into the 20th century, and numerous memorials worldwide have been dedicated to him.

Daniel Boone was a man, a real man...so at least the song goes. In reality, Boone was an explorer, frontiersman, and pioneer who blazed the Wilderness Road trail from Virginia to Kentucky through the Appalachian Mountains. He fought during the American Revolution, was elected to the Virginia Assembly, and of course, became a legend in his own time.

Boone was an authentic trailblazer. The Appalachian Mountains form a natural barrier to east-west travel. There are only five ways to travel to the west across this mountain chain from New York to Georgia. And only three natural interior breaks would allow animal-powered travel without great engineering works. These were the Gaps of the Allegheny, the Kittanning Paths in Pennsylvania, the Cumberland Narrows in northwestern Maryland (host to Nemacolin's Path), the Cumberland Gap in the four-state region of North Carolina and Virginia on the east side, and through the gap between Tennessee and Kentucky.

While late 19th and 20th-century technologies would later bridge the mountain chain in other places, these all required significant civil engineering works to make a roadbed past the barrier range geologists classify as the ridge-and-valley Appalachians. Settlers from Pennsylvania tended to migrate south along the Great Wagon Road through the Great Appalachian Valley and Shenandoah Valley.

Daniel Boone was from Pennsylvania and migrated south with his family along this road. From an early age, Boone was one of the long hunters who hunted and trapped among the Native American nations along the western frontiers of Virginia, so-called because of the long time they spent away from home on hunts in the wilderness. Boone would sometimes be gone for months and even years before returning home from his hunting expeditions.

Boone recommended three essentials for a pioneer: "A good gun, a good horse, and a good wife." He also would need a strong body, a sharp ax, and good luck. Another essential was salt. Before 1776, salt had to be shipped into the Thirteen Colonies from the West Indies at great expense. It was the only meat preservative available for men on the move and Kentucky had an extra lure with its large salt brine lakes near what is today the community of Boonesborough, Kentucky. The many "salt licks" of Kentucky are today reflected in the many place names in the state that use the words "lick" or "licking."

In March 1775, Boone, along with 35 axmen, cut a trail from Long Island in Kingsport, Tennessee, through the forests and mountains to Kentucky. It was a rough mud trail, hardly more than a path. The Transylvania Company had obtained title to Kentucky from the Cherokee and Iroquois. The Shawnee chief Cornstalk, defeated in Dunmore's War, had promised at the Treaty of Camp Charlotte in October 1774 that his tribe would no longer hunt or claim land south of the Ohio River in Kentucky.

Notwithstanding this promise, the Shawnee viewed Boone and other settlers as invaders. On March 24, 1775, Boone and his party were only 15 miles (24 km) from their final destination of the Kentucky River when they camped for the night. Just before daybreak, a group of Shawnees, slinging tomahawks, attacked the sleeping men. Some of Boone's party were killed and a few were wounded, but most escaped into the woods. Boone regrouped his men and managed to drive off the hostile Shawnee. The party did, however, lose some of their horses.

Jacques-Yves Cousteau was a French naval officer, explorer, conservationist, filmmaker, innovator, scientist, photographer, author, and researcher who studied the sea and all forms of life in the ocean. He co-developed the Aqua-Lung, pioneered marine conservation, and was a member of the Académie Française.

As a French Naval officer, Cousteau blazed a trail and captured people's imaginations when it came to exploring life under the sea. His ship *Calypso* was retro-fitted to meet his exploratory demands. *The Undersea World of Jacques Cousteau* was a famous and popular TV program in the late 60s and early 70s.

Cousteau described his underwater world research in a series of books, perhaps the most successful being his first book, *The Silent World: A Story of Undersea Discovery and Adventure*, published in 1953. Cousteau also directed films, most notably the documentary adaptation of the book, *The Silent World*, which won a Palme d'Or at the

1956 Cannes Film Festival. He remained the only person to win a Palme d'Or for a documentary film, until Michael Moore won the award in 2004 for *Fahrenheit 9/11*.

Juan Ponce de Leon, more commonly referred to as Ponce de Leon, is mostly thought of as the explorer dedicated to finding the legendary Fountain of Youth. Leon was a Spanish explorer and conquistador best known for leading the first official European expedition to Florida and serving as the first governor of Puerto Rico.

He was born in Santervás de Campos, Valladolid, Spain, in 1474. While little is known about his family and upbringing, we know he was of noble birth and served in the Spanish military at a young age.

Leon first came to the Americas as a "gentleman volunteer" with Christopher Columbus's second expedition in 1493. By appointment under the Spanish Crown, he became the first governor of Puerto Rico. However, as a result of an ongoing feud and a series of legal actions with Christopher Columbus's son Diego, he lost the position and Diego became the new governor. Following the advice of King Ferdinand, Leon left Puerto Rico to explore more of the Caribbean Sea.

In 1513, Leon led an expedition to what he named La Florida and was reinstated as governor of Puerto Rico. Although modern historians claim there is no supporting evidence that Leon was ever searching for the Fountain of Youth, there is also no evidence that he was not. Let God be the judge.

Norwegian explorer Roald Engelbregt Gravning Amundsen was born in 1872. When he was 15 years old, Amundsen was enthralled by reading the narratives of Sir John Franklin's overland Arctic expeditions. Amundsen wrote, "I read them with a fervid fascination which has shaped the whole course of my life."

His mother wanted him to avoid the family maritime trade and encouraged him to become a doctor, a promise that Amundsen kept until his mother died when he was 21. He promptly quit his university studies for a life at sea.

Amundsen went on to lead an expedition to the Antarctic and thereby his discovery of the South Pole in 1911. Years later, he led another team to the North Pole. In addition, Amundsen was the first to go through the Northwest Passage, a route that begins in the Arctic Ocean and ends in the Pacific Ocean. Amundsen is one of four men considered leaders of the Heroic Age of Antarctic Exploration. He disappeared while taking part in a rescue mission for the airship *Italia* in 1928.

In 1953, New Zealander Edmund Hillary and fellow mountaineer Tenzing Norgay of Nepal became the first two individuals to summit Mt. Everest. Hillary became interested in climbing when he was 16, following a 1935 school trip to Mount Ruapehu. After this trip, he showed more interest in tramping, a style of hiking and backpacking in New Zealand, than in studying and announced that he "wanted to see the world."

Tenzing Norgay was born in Khumbu, Nepal. As a local climber, Norgay had experience in climbing Mt. Everest when the two joined forces. In 1952, Norgay took part in the two Swiss expeditions led by Edouard Wyss-Dunant (spring) and Gabriel Chevalley (autumn). These were the first serious attempts to climb Everest from the southern (Nepalese) side, after two previous US and British reconnaissance expeditions in 1950 and 1951.

Raymond Lambert and Norgay reached a height of about 8,595 meters (28,199 feet) on the southeast ridge, setting a new climbing altitude record. The expedition opened up a new route on Everest that was successfully climbed the next year.

In 1953, Norgay took part in John Hunt's expedition; Tenzing had previously been to Everest six times (and Hunt three). A member of that team was Edmund Hillary, who had a near-miss falling into a crevasse. He was saved from hitting bottom by Norgay's prompt action in securing the rope using his ice ax, which led Hillary to consider him the climbing partner of choice for any future summit attempt.

The Hunt expedition totaled over 400 people, including 362 porters, 20 Sherpa guides, and 10,000 pounds (4,500 kg) of baggage. Like many such expeditions, this was a team effort. Considering the equipment they had to use, the lack of logistical data, and limited resources, the accomplishment was nothing less than miraculous.

Another notable feat that Hillary accomplished, in addition to his Mount Everest achievement, is that he also ventured to both the North and South Poles, which made him the first man to reach all three landmarks.

In 1978, Reinhold Messner, a modern-day Italian contemporary of Hillary, was the first man to successfully summit Mount Everest with no oxygen to supplement his climb.

Why is this "first" so significant? Mount Everest near its summit can have weather extremes, deep cold, and steep icy slopes. Quick, accurate decision-making may be needed. Without enough oxygen during the ascent, people cannot think clearly. At the summit itself, a person's oxygen intake is less than one-third that at sea level.

Messner is considered to be among the five greatest mountain climbers of all time. He is also the first man to climb fourteen mountains that are at least 8,000 meters (26,247 feet) high. The lowest mountain he climbed was Gasherbrum II at the China-Pakistan Karakoram range, its height, 8,034 meters (26,358 feet).

Footnote: a Nepalese mountain climber has now climbed Mount Everest a record 24 times — and he is hoping to do it one more time before he retires. Kami Rita Sherpa, 49, has been climbing Everest since 1994.

CHAPTER 9

The Resilient Rulers

R esilient Rulers (RR) are passionate and purposefully driven catalysts of change. They are visionaries in clarity of thought, with the ability to see situations and circumstances as they truly are – mere setbacks and obstacles to be overcome.

RRs have the vision, strength, endurance, and commitment to stay the course. The take-charge leadership skills of an RR may be hard to spot in good times, but become readily apparent and visual as their character traits and "true grit" are forged in times of great hardships and adversity.

When the time comes for decisiveness, they rise to the occasion and their results are nothing less than noble and great. One example is the effort of Molly Brown, an American socialite and philanthropist who, following the sinking of the Titanic, brazenly impelled the captain of the lifeboat to return to the debris field and look for survivors.

RRs attract the attention of the masses. They are lauded by their followers, canonized by the media, and, in most instances, achieve worldwide recognition and acclaim by virtue of their leadership, resilience, and purposefully driven lives. RRs make the headlines, dominate social media, and create history. RRs are appreciated at every level of leadership. Witnessing an RR struggle against all odds is inspiring in itself.

What role do RRs play in society?

- RRs inspire resilience in others.

- RRs teach us how to overcome obstacles.

- RRs motivate change within us.

- RRs inspire through other virtues such as patience, calmness, toughness, and tenacity.

- RRs think on their feet; they make decisions independently and spontaneously.

There are several ways to spot an RR; here are a few characteristics that define them:

- RRs take calculated risks.

- RRs are not risk-seeking.

- RRs are mentors, trainers, or teachers.

- RRs take the responsibility to prepare the team.

- RR leaders seek feedback.

- RRs love learning.

- RRs are proactive and adaptable.

- RRs act decisively.

All great rulers have something quirky about themselves. Winston Churchill was known for walking around his home naked, while Abraham Lincoln slept diagonally, perhaps because beds in his day were too short for his 6'4" physique. Honest to a fault, Lincoln is also remembered for walking six miles to repay a three-cent overpayment, a bit unusual in these times.

The Old Testament introduced Solomon, who was visited by God in a dream following a sacrifice Solomon had offered. In the dream, he was asked what gift he would have bestowed upon him; all he needed do was to ask. There are many who, under similar circumstances, may have chosen extrinsic rewards such as gold, silver, fame, fortune, or a long and healthy life.

It is significant to recognize that Solomon chose an intrinsic trait that originates within the heart. A trait of which all noblemen seek. The quality is wisdom, and it would become the distinguishing trait, a household phrase, and a compliment toward all that recognize and appreciate good judgment.

Leadership has been defined as a process through which a person influences and motivates others to get involved in accomplishing a particular task. Although universally accepted, this single definition fails to define the particular paths and ways of people deemed as great leaders. All great leaders generally have one thing in common, they all have something unique or a bit quirky about themselves, yet they still achieve greatness and lead people toward innovation, new ideologies, and a fresh perspective.

Since the dawning of civilization, the masses have been led by effective leaders. Such men and women have been responsible for ushering people into a new and more modern world. Although times have changed, the contributions of these great leaders cannot be forgotten.

And although practices and ways of doing things are different as well, the ways and methods of these great leaders cannot be overlooked. What made them great might still be applicable in today's day and age. Here is a look at some of the greatest and most resilient leaders of all time and what made them successful.

Mahatma Gandhi — Mohandas Karamchand Gandhi, aka Mahatma Gandhi, was born under ordinary circumstances, yet lived his life with a determination to excel at whatever he did. Following law school in London, he grew to become the single most influential Indian freedom advocate and threat to colonial rule in history. His tactic of non-violence protests through civil disobedience led his home country of India to freedom in 1947. The character traits he is most remembered for were his resilience, knowledge, people skills, motivational creativity, and leading by example.

George Washington — George Washington, known as the founding father of the United States of America, was a leader of the American Revolution and the first president of the U.S. He was a true visionary whose vision has endured for more than 200 years. What made Washington great was his foresight, vision, strategic planning, and his ability to lead people to success.

Abraham Lincoln — The 16th president of the United States and arguably the most revered and respected U.S. President our country has ever had. He was in office during the American Civil War, where he kept the people together and was the linchpin in keeping our nation from fragmenting. Lincoln officially ended slavery in the U.S. by signing the Emancipation Proclamation. His greatest traits were his determination, persistence, beliefs, and courage.

Adolf Hitler — Although despised throughout the world, Adolf Hitler was a great leader. After becoming Chancellor of Germany in 1933, he was responsible for one of the greatest economic and military expansions the world has ever seen. He successfully invaded more than ten countries with his brilliant strategy and meticulous planning. His oratory skills, propaganda, and planning made him a leader par excellence.

Muhammad — A passionate leader of Islam and the single most influential person responsible for Islam's growth in and around Arabia. His efforts united a chaotic society in the name of morality and humanity and helped lead his people out of severe persecution and mistreatment. He also led his followers on several migrations and victories in wars against armies much larger than theirs. Islam is now the second-largest and fastest-growing religion in the world today. His greatest leadership qualities were his courage, leading by example, motivational approach, persistence, and decision-making.

Nelson Mandela — Nelson Mandela was the first South African president elected in fully democratic elections. Mandela was also the main player in the country's anti-apartheid movements, which resulted in him serving a lengthy prison sentence. This did not stop Mandela. In fact, it motivated him to devote his life to uniting his country, which he successfully managed to do so after his release from an almost 30-year prison sentence. His main characteristics were determination, persistence, focus, and will.

Julius Caesar — Easily one of the greatest military leaders of all time, Caesar was also one of the best political leaders the world has ever seen. He led several campaigns with numerous victories and was single-handedly responsible for the expansion of the Roman Empire. He was also responsible for reforming the Roman government, thus laying the foundation for a great empire. His greatest traits were his decisiveness, boldness, eagerness, motivation, opportunism, and strategic planning.

Fidel Castro — Castro was the leader of the Cuban Revolution and later became the Prime Minister of Cuba. He was the President of Cuba from 1976 to 2008. He endured many crises, invasions, and assassination attempts and took them in stride. His vision for Cuba still stands, and he proved to be an effective leader and commander. His traits of courage, strategy, hiring the right people, and dissemination of duties made him the leader he was.

Winston Churchill — Prime Minister of Great Britain from 1940 to 1945, Churchill led the nation against Nazi Germany during World War II. He teamed up with allies, which consequently led to the defeat and downfall of Hitler. His tenure as the British Prime Minister was in a time of fear and destruction caused by Hitler and his allies. Churchill was known for his fearlessness, determination, unyielding perseverance, and undying devotion to his goal.

Building Respect and Loyalty
Throughout human history, mankind has witnessed many great rulers. Some conquered almost half of the world, while others led their nations in times of great crisis. These leaders were able to serve both the needs of the people and the needs of the state.

The following individuals are on the top ten rankings according to respect and their followers' loyalty. These rulers were responsible for changing the course of history. Each of these individuals lived up to the definition of greatness.

Here is the list of the top ten greatest rulers of all time.

10. **Suleiman** — This individual was known by several names, including The Magnificent, The Sultan, and many more. He ruled the Ottoman Empire for more than 60 years, the longest tenure recorded. Before his rule, the Ottoman Empire, which spread across the Middle East and regions of Southeastern Europe, was not progressing

rapidly. But with the advent of Suleiman I, all social, economic, cultural, and political spheres showed rapid growth. His reign over the empire was considered to be the golden age for the people.

9. **Cyrus II of Persia** — The greatest ruler in the history of the Persian Empire, Cyrus II, was yet another highly skilled, brave, and atypical person. During his reign, the entire empire witnessed several revolutionary reforms that were introduced. He gave human rights and all other minority rights priority. He ruled the empire for more than 30 years and added many territories to his empire. The countries today of Israel, Iran, and many other Middle East areas were included in his empire. The inclusion of big countries and areas in his empire was primarily due to the special and tactical military strategies he adopted.

8. **Joseph Stalin** — The pride of the Russians, Joseph Stalin, was responsible for bringing the October Revolution in Russia with great support from the local masses. During his period, Russia showed rapid growth in industrial, science, agricultural, and political influence. Despite what people today think about him, and seen from a neutral and unbiased perspective, Stalin is indeed one of the greatest rulers of all time. He transformed a struggling and weak nation into one of the strongest superpowers in the world. Additionally, Stalin stood against Hitler and prevented him from taking control of all of Europe.

7. **Asoka the Great** — The greatest Indian emperor of all time was Asoka, sometimes spelled Ashoka. He gained control over the entire Indian, Pakistani, and Afghanistan states, an exceptionally large area to be conquered. His huge success was due to his extraordinary abilities in crafting and implementing military strategies. He also introduced numerous reforms and initiated an everlasting construction process in India.

6. **Adolf Hitler** — There is no doubt that this man was responsible for many deaths. But, at the same time, the abilities he possessed empowered him to conquer almost all of Europe. Although Hitler is most recognized as an egotistical mass murder, he was to some Germans a gifted strategist, and one of the greatest leaders in the history of Germany. Before him, Germany was facing many economic and social problems, and the country was on the road to decline. With the arrival of Hitler, Germany experienced a golden age, the glory of which may never be forgotten by the Germans. Whether you speak of technological advancements or economic superstructures, no doubt Hitler improved everything in Germany.

5. **Genghis Khan** — Remembered as the most brutal Emperor in world history, Genghis Khan is in our number five spot. Although he mercilessly slaughtered his enemies, when it comes to establishing a strong Empire, his abilities and achievements cannot be denied. He was the founder of the Mongol Empire, considered to be the most dominant and powerful force in the world. He possessed excellent legislation abilities, and during his reign several Asian tribes were gathered under one banner.

4. **Caesar** — Also known by the name of Augustus, Caesar was the first ruler of the Roman Empire. Ruling the empire for more than 30 years, his strategies in battle, emphasis on democracy, and establishing a government and laws by the voice of the people were noble and great. Under his reign, Rome gained control of several powerful empires. It is said that he never lost a single war. In terms of lawmaking, he amended countless baseless laws and regulations that were prevalent before him. But at the same time, he developed many enemies within his senate, who later murdered him.

3. **Queen Elizabeth I** — Known as the virgin queen, Queen Elizabeth I ruled England and Ireland for many years. Her life is indeed one of the best examples for women who think that they can never rule. The reason behind her name as the Virgin Queen was that she never married because she never wanted to depend on a king. During her rule, she protected her people from many outside forces and united them under one flag. Due to her excellent legislation abilities, she earned a lot of respect and love from her people. She had also encouraged the use of science, knowledge, and exploration.

2. **Napoleon** — Best known as Emperor Napoleon, he is France's greatest ruler and one of the greatest rulers in history. He conquered many European regions and areas, primarily because of his calculated military tactics and superior strategies. The legislation and lawmaking which he initiated are still remembered. He set examples of strong administration and legislation for the whole world. He never considered himself a conqueror or invader, but rather as a person making a nation of independent and free people.

1. **Alexander the Great** — The ruler who conquered more than half of the world. Alexander was appointed ruler at an incredibly young age after the murder of his father. Being a student of the great philosopher Aristotle gave him many insights into politics. He won all the major and minor battles which he fought. During his reign, Alexander gained control of the Persian Empire, which was the most difficult to conquer in those times. He established a new and stronger Macedonian Empire during his rule. In short, his empire covered all the major areas from Europe to India, which is indeed the greatest sovereign achievement in history.

CHAPTER 10

The Fall of Despair

In the early 1990s, an American clothing line swept the athletic world almost as fast as the goddess of victory herself, Nike. The branding foundation for its exponential growth was a two-word phrase created by race car driver Brian Simo in 1989 that would eventually become the mantra of extreme sports.

Although the phrase was only two words and six letters, the breadth of its reach was enormous. Due to various mishaps, the clothing line was not sustained. However, the brand survived as an energy drink and is currently the World Extreme Cage fighting (WEC) official promotion beverage. The phrase is "No Fear."

Fear can be either a disabling emotion or an enabling emotion. According to Christopher Ingraham of the Washington Post, at least half of the world population has some sort of phobia that hinders their functional ability.

Overall, fear of public speaking is America's biggest phobia (25.3%), while 7.9 percent fear clowns more than ghosts (7.6 percent). Zombies are officially the scarier of all three at 8.9 percent. On a political note: Democrats are significantly more likely to fear bugs, snakes, and other animals, as well as blood and needles.

For many of us, our childhood, our upbringing, and setbacks in life have created a false self-image of who we think we are, what we are capable of accomplishing, and what we can become. Fear can be a powerfully debilitating and inhibiting force that can lead its possessor on a downward spiral to regret, self-pity, and depression.

On the other hand, fear can influence us to kneel in prayer and supplication in search of higher meaning and greater faith, wisdom, and understanding.

Fear can have a controlling impact in our lives. It can influence our progression, regression, or stagnation in our journey in life.

Fear can whisper we are inferior and incapable of rising above our perceived imperfections to pursue a higher purpose in life. It can erode personal progress, self-esteem, and spiritual progression. If we allow it to linger, fear can rob us of our very birthright.

Apathy is a close cousin of fear. It, too, bears a tremendous opportunity cost and a negative consequence with its victims. Apathy is mediocrity personified. An apathetic person has neither faith, hope, charity, nor purpose. When apathy is abundant, possibilities cease, grace becomes superfluous, and the door of depression is wide open for business.

Wikipedia defines apathy as a "lack of feeling, emotion, interest, and concern." Apathy is a state of indifference or suppressing emotions such as excitement, motivation, or passion. An apathetic person lacks interest in emotional content, social interaction, spiritual progression, philosophical pursuits, physical fitness, and the world around them. If you go with them to the ice cream parlor, the chances are they will order Vanilla. Why? Because it is familiar and comfortable, they know what they are getting. Why take a chance?

The apathetic person lacks purpose, self-worth, or meaning in their life. They tend to be insensible, sluggish, and lethargic, mostly because they have convinced themselves they lack the level of skill required to compete or improve. It may also result from perceiving no challenge at all (e.g., the challenge is irrelevant to them, or conversely, they have learned helplessness).

Apathy may be a sign of more specific mental problems, such as schizophrenia or dementia. However, apathy is something that all people face in some capacity. It is a natural response to disappointment, dejection, and stress. As a response mechanism, apathy is a way to forget about these negative feelings. This type of common apathy is usually short term. If it becomes a long-term, or even a life-long, state, deeper social and psychological issues will most likely be present.

The third and final negative emotion that can erode our self-esteem and hamstring our progression is doubt. It is averse to optimism and it has the power to distort our spiritual peace of mind and deflect our spiritual vision.

The Sea of Galilee, located in the northeastern quadrant of Israel, was a landmark and venue for many of the miracles and lessons performed and taught by Jesus Christ. One of His most poignant teaching moments, as recorded in The New Testament, was between Jesus and his senior apostle, Peter. The lesson emphasized the essential nature of faith and the limiting and controlling effect doubt can have in our lives.

In Mathew 14:23-32. we read,

> "And when he had sent the multitudes away, he went up into a mountain apart to pray. And

when the evening was come, he was there alone. But the ship was now in the midst of the sea, tossed with waves: for the wind was contrary. And in the fourth watch of the night Jesus went unto them, walking on the sea. And when the disciples saw him walking on the sea, they were troubled, saying, It is a spirit; and they cried out for fear. But straightway Jesus spake unto them, saying, Be of good cheer; it is I; be not afraid. And Peter answered him and said, Lord, if it be thou, bid me come unto thee on the water. And he said, Come. And when Peter was come down out of the ship, he walked on the water, to go to Jesus. But when he saw the wind boisterous, he was afraid; and beginning to sink, he cried, saying, Lord, save me. And immediately Jesus stretched forth his hand, and caught him, and said unto him, O thou of little faith, wherefore didst thou doubt? And when they were come into the ship, the wind ceased."

Fear, Apathy, and Doubt combined create FAD. This particular state of mind will not pass quickly, nor does it breed enthusiasm. This type of fad, if left untreated, has the potential impact to drain the individual of possibilities, fulfillment, and joy that comes from self-realization, purpose, and humanitarian service. Unfortunately, FAD is not easily overpowered.

Overcoming the influence of these restrictive emotions will be a steep grade, yet the journey need not be taken alone. The encouragement, praise, and recognition you receive as you make this journey will come from those who love you and those who have made the journey themselves.

The Underdog

Who among us has not witnessed and applauded the underdog? The person who, against all odds (including groupthink, criticism, and opposition from multiple parties), presses forward and succeeds. In doing so, they shatter public opinion and destroy the credibility of pessimists who would prefer seeing the individual fail and wallow in the angst of defeat.

Consider the obscure Jamaican Bobsled Team, that against all odds for success, competed in a sport that was unconnected to the country they were representing. Then there was Eddie the Eagle, the long-distance ski jumper, from Great Britain! There are no ski jumps in Britain.

Hollywood is always quick to capitalize on long-odds sports competitors. Indeed, the thrill of victory against all odds is alluring and praiseworthy. Conversely, the agony of defeat may be even more alluring and drive higher viewership ratings. There are some in society who enjoy watching others get pummeled or lose their lives. While this is sadistic entertainment, it gives them something to talk about.

History has shown that spreading the news about death and carnage is profitable. If you are not sure, just turn on the news. Who can forget the *Wide World of Sports* television program in the early 70s? The opening showcased the thrill of victory and "the agony of defeat." The latter phrase was illustrated with the image of Vinko Bogataj, a Slovenian Ski Jumper in a Ski Flying event in Oberstdorf, West Germany, when he blew the takeoff and flipped end over end like a ragdoll toward a group of spectators.

What made these two expressions – No Fear and "the agony of defeat" – so popular? Why does winning in our society seem to matter so much? Why does physical, mental, emotional, and spiritual superiority attract so many watchful eyes? Why is the need to excel so powerful and the sense of failure so devastating to our psyche?

Why do some of us spend our whole lives striving to reach the summit of personal achievement and give up all hope when the goal is unattained? Why is sub-performance so impactfully detrimental to our state of mind? Why do some excel while others have far less success? What does in "the zone" really mean?

The distinction and recognition of a Noble and Great One is predicated upon the fulfillment of a superior pre-disposition and realization that their gifts and talents are bestowed for the benefit of humanity, rather than the aggrandizement of self.

This self-realization of giftedness does not come overnight. Rather, it comes gradually as the NGO replaces counterfeit impressions of who they may think they are and what they may think they are capable or incapable of becoming. The self-realization of an NGO does not come from the accomplishment itself. Instead, it comes from a deep appreciation for the refining journey and acknowledgment from where their accomplishment came.

CHAPTER 11

The Rise of Hope

In the world today, there are a plethora of opportunities that provide a proving ground for determining the giftedness within each one of us. Those who discover their gifts and talents early in life can clearly progress further and influence more people with their unique giftedness and achievements.

Genetics or human nature, combined with nurture or upbringing, are two of the most influential forces impacting our self-image and shaping our views of the world around us. These two forces, coupled with key life experiences at pivotal moments of our journey through life, are the key ingredients that foster and encourage the emergence and development of an NGO. The influences and life experiences are the sparks that ignite the passion and power of the NGO to overcome difficulties and acquire greater strength and continual improvement of self and humanity.

Courage, commitment, passion, and purpose are all by-products of self-realization and discovering our identity, purpose, and potential. These are the motivating characteristics that elevate the gifted athlete from good to great and the accomplished intellectual from brilliance to genius. This fire in the belly is the enabling force found within them that fuels the affinity toward passion versus passivity, domination versus complacency, and lifelessness versus an active and purposeful life of sacrifice, obedience, discovery, self-realization, and service to others.

The nurture and nature of the early developmental years of our lives create the soil from which our self-image is formed and developed. For some of us, the soil of our upbringing may have been encumbered by noxious weeds of defeat, disillusionment, apathy, and pessimism. On the other hand, others may have enjoyed the fertile soil from which self-improvement, personal achievement, faith, and optimism in facing and overcoming challenges, setbacks, and difficulties flourish.

Although the abundance of disparity between these two forces will have a bearing on self-image, it is essential to remember, "it's not about the proportions, it's what's in the glass that matters most."

This concept of rulership is eternal. It began in the pre-mortal existence as spirit children of a loving Father in Heaven that created us each for a special purpose. It continues throughout our lifetime, and it will continue into the eternities. It begins with wonderment as we interpret the world around us. In time we learn to crawl. Next, we learn to stand and eventually begin to walk. At that point, a child's personality is more easily identified, and the role of parenting is in full swing.

Our faith and belief in our earthly parents, their love, and their personal examples encourage and entice the infant to take baby steps and strive to become their own persona. Once their roots have been healthily established, the child begins to recognize his or her own uniqueness. Impressions and experiences encourage them to discover their unique gifts, talents, and abilities. Eventually, they leave their nest parents and become contributing members of society.

If parents are wise, they teach their children lessons of independence, interdependence, team-building with others, and dependence on a Heavenly Father who is ever mindful and always ready to support and aid them in their time of need. This teaches children humility, respect, honor, and gratitude for their earthly parents and reverence for their heavenly parents. If we do not learn to rule our earthly home effectively, it will be difficult to rule our heavenly home in the future.

Although a ruler may be destined for greatness, he or she becomes as such, line upon line, precept upon precept, until their role in society becomes clear to them. Once the NGO acknowledges their nobility and bandwidth for greatness, he or she will innately and instinctively extend themselves willingly, compassionately, and purposefully for the benefit of humanity.

CHAPTER 12

Put on the Armor of God

The history of the world teaches that societies built upon noble principles, and that are led by virtuous and just rulers who make resolute decisions based on what is right or good for the community and the individual, receive God's approval and, more often than not, enjoy peace, harmony, and prosperity.

When we inhale those blessings and judge others by proportions of the haves and have nots, our head expands creating room for degrading thoughts to enter that will eventually dissuade us from brother kindness and humility. Additionally, our dependency upon God wanes, and pride in one's own accomplishments and possessions take priority over the things that matter the most, such as our relationships, helping others, and remembering the source from where all blessings flow.

Whenever we rely on our own strength and seek our own agenda, we cross the line from selflessness to selfishness and forget who we are, why we are here, and where we are going.

Wars are often ignited by pride. They have existed for thousands of years, even before the dawn of mankind. The Book of Revelations attests. "there was even war in

Heaven and one-third of the hosts of Heaven were banished and cast down to this earth." (Revelations 12:9)

The number of lives taken in wars is in the billions. The lives that were lost in the War in Heaven was likely in the trillions.

What causes mankind to abandon nobility and compassion for one another, allow hearts to wax cold, and wage war against fellow brothers and sisters?

Like a Roaring Lion

What causes men and women to despise one another? What is the root cause that man's love can grow cold between one another, resulting in conflict?

The root cause of most wars can be summed up in a single 5-letter word; that word is PRIDE.

> P stands for power. It was power that fueled Lucifer's expulsion from the heavenly presence of the Father. It was power that incited his anger against Michael the Archangel and the hosts of heaven. Power was the enticement to challenge the Father and challenge our redeemer. The allure of power was the motivation behind Satan's temptation to convince Adam and Eve; it was one of the tenants he used in bringing about the fall and expulsion of Adam and Eve from the garden.
>
> R stands for rage, an emotion that represents anger personified. Those that rage cannot see clearly, nor can they think intelligently. "For behold, at that day shall he rage in the hearts of the children of men, and stir them up to anger against that which is good." (2 NE 28:20 Book of Mormon)

I stands for ignorance. Throughout the ages, many have suffered from an ignorant comment, a misinformed decision, or an unfounded sense of superiority over another. You may recall the warning from the Ghost of Christmas Day in the beloved book *Scrooge*. Upon opening his robe to reveal two young children inside, he declared, "This one is Ignorance." About the other, he stated, "And this one is Want." He then added, "Of the two, beware of Ignorance."

D stands for deceit. Those that harbor pride do so because they have a strong need to be right and in control of the outcome. They justify their actions due to feelings of entitlement, and they will say, do, and manipulate others for what they perceive is their due reward.

Deceivers are often difficult to recognize; they are often labeled incorrectly as opportunists when in reality they are *shyster's incognito*. The basis for their callous treatment of others, and their love of self, versus their love of God and His children, is seeded in revenge, self-righteousness, and self-glory.

The E stands for envy. Those that are prideful are rarely thankful for what they have. Rather than trying to keep up with the Joneses, they desire to beat the Joneses no matter what it takes. They celebrate the failures of others and praise themselves rather than thanking their heavenly benefactor.

A More Excellent Way

Few individuals throughout history can rival the commitment, hardships, and suffering that the Apostle

Paul endured for the sake of Christianity. His life was a testament that no matter how far the pendulum may swing, God's love is omnipotent, He is involved in the details of our lives, and, as the Prodigal Son reveals, He is quick to forgive and celebrate our return home.

Such was the life of the Apostle Paul, a once zealous persecutor, home-breaker, and an executioner of all those who professed a belief in Jesus Christ. A wayward son of God, who saw the light (both literally and figuratively). He changed his course 180 degrees to become one of the greatest Christian advocates, disciples, and proselytizing missionaries of all time.

Paul traveled further, remained longer, and endured more adversity than any other missionary in Western religion. His teachings were so powerful and influential that they comprise one-third of the New Testament.

Paul devoted the majority of his life to spreading the gospel of Jesus Christ and making restitution for the damage and atrocities he had committed against the children of God.

In the midst of a blinding conversion on the road to Damascus, with a heart and soul grieved by the recognition, inexpressible guilt, and remorse in realizing the numerous atrocities, grievous sins, and death sentences he ordered against the Son of God and His followers came the repentant cry of allegiance and restitution, "Who Art Thou, Lord? What wilt thou have me do?"

As a Pharisee, Paul would have been trained to follow 613 mosaic commandments, the first two commandments being 1) love the Lord thy God and 2) to love your fellow man as you would love yourself.

What a difference would it make if our society chose to honor and obey these two commandments. How different the world would be!

The mosaic commandments were separated into two categories, 365 positive commandments on how to act (one for each day of the year) and 248 negative commandments on how we should refrain from acting. Collectively all these laws are comprised in the Jewish canon of scripture known as the Torah.

Now, imagine having lived your entire life from birth to age 30, striving to interpret, obey, and judge others by the manner and extent to which those around you recognize, obey, or choose to disobey these commandments. Would your image of Christianity be heightened or diminished if your inbred and ingrained belief were the true Messiah and Savior of your people would return one day in the future to thrash your enemies and restore justice to your people?

Now imagine you become aware that one of your own people is promoting, challenging, and in essence, downgrading your beliefs.

Next, imagine you had been given Roman authority and capacity to exercise capital punishment against all those you deem are in direct opposition to your religious beliefs and justifiably in opposition to the will of the Roman Empire. You then exercise that authority by entering Christian homes located in the very heart of the Roman Empire's largest metropolitan cities and drag these Christians from their homes into the streets in broad daylight and execute them.

How could you ever believe that such a person — having such hatred for other beliefs, thoughts, and actions — could reverse and spend his last breath passionately and enduringly defending the very person he had spent the first half of his life desecrating?

It would take a _ _ _ _ _ _ _, you fill in the blanks..., yes, a miracle!

The conversion process was swift, even as a two-edged sword. It came by way of divine angelic intervention.

Although Paul's repentance process was relatively brief, it was resolute when we consider the distances he would travel, the suffering he would endure, and the restitution he would make for his sins against the sons and daughters of God. It would take a visit from the long-awaited Messiah himself, the author and originator of the single greatest catalyst of change. It would take Jesus Christ.

Christianity is, at present, the largest religion in the world. Its followers revere the New Testament as the word of God and its didactic counsel as the standard for how Christians should live their lives. For those who have not read this book, its central figures are Jesus Christ, for whom the faith is named, and the disciples He specifically called and ordained to join him in sharing His and His Father's gospel.

As a disciple of Christ, Paul spoke openly and frequently regarding the virtues and attributes of nobility as taught by the Master. There was one virtue he taught which overshadowed all the other virtues, a quality he introduced as a More Excellent Way. The quality he refers to is charity. Its composition is the embodiment of multiple virtues that we all must learn to incorporate in our lives to bear the title of being a Christian.

There are 13 Pauline Epistles recorded in the New Testament, nearly one-third of the volume of scripture found in this holy writ. Paul's epistle to the saints in

Corinth, found in 1 Corinthians chapter 13, is relatively short, yet each verse evokes deep import.

Charity is at the heart of Christlike love and empathy for others. The charitable person asks what he can do to help another, rather than label, cling to self-righteous judgment, or withhold forgiveness. Charity tempers our words, motivates change, and magnifies our efforts. It is an unconditional love for a brother or sister that has fallen from the path of righteousness.

Paul opens his epistle to the Saints in Corinthians using these three verses:

> Verse 1 – Though I speak with the tongues of men and of angels, and have not charity, I am become as sounding brass, or a tinkling cymbal.
>
> Verse 2 – And though I have the gift of prophecy, and understand all mysteries, and all knowledge; and though I have all faith, so that I could remove mountains, and have not charity, I am nothing.
>
> Verse 3 – And though I bestow all my goods to feed the poor, and though I give my body to be burned, and have not charity, it profited me nothing.

Not knowing what factors were at play in the mind of Paul in choosing these exact words, but to anyone that knew what Paul had been through, they had to have been interpreted as a clarion warning and a rebuke to the self-righteous, the casual Christian and the Average Joe Parishioner who feel they are doing enough by going to church. Either way you interpret these verses, the message is that charity is the More Excellent Way and without it, our service to others will have little to no merit.

Charity goes beyond brotherly kindness; charity is a soul-searching and soul-saving force in the universe. Charity is a refining virtue that can free us from the incarcerating bonds of the natural man and draw us toward the liberating, unconditional, and endlessly forgiving outstretched arms of the Savior. Faith, hope, charity, and love may lead us to Christ, but charity is the surest way of knowing Christ.

Charity has the power to change our very nature. It is essential to our salvation and the litmus test of Christianity. Without charity, we are non-practicing, noninfluential, and ineffective Christians. Without charity, we are strangers to Christ. Without charity, we are nothing.

In this relatively short chapter, Paul delivers the embodiment of nobility by referencing a single word, without which our ability to invite and influence change in others and bring them to Christ is futile. It was the driving force behind the creation. It was the foundation for the plan of salvation and was the defining force behind the greatest sacrifice in all eternity, the Atonement.

The following verses represent the qualities of charity and the virtues we must learn to cultivate in order to become charitable toward ourselves and our fellowman:

> "Charity suffereth long, and is kind; charity envieth not; charity vaunteth not itself, is not puffed up, doth not behave itself unseemly, seeketh not her own, is not easily provoked, thinketh no evil; Rejoiceth not in iniquity, but rejoiceth in the truth; beareth all things, believeth all things, hopeth all things, endureth all things. Charity never faileth: but whether

there be prophecies, they shall fail; whether there be tongues, they shall cease; whether there be knowledge, it shall vanish away. For we know in part, and we prophesy in part. But when that which is perfect is come, then that which is in part shall be done away. When I was a child, I spake as a child, I understood as a child, I thought as a child: but when I became a man, I put away childish things. For now we see through a glass, darkly; but then face to face: now I know in part; but then shall I know even as also I am known. And now abideth faith, hope, charity, these three; but the greatest of these is charity." (1 Corinthians 4-13)

This change in wisdom, stature, or disposition will not come without sacrifice, daily self-assessment, and chastening. Ralph Waldo Emerson said it best; "Sow a thought and you reap an action; sow an action and you reap a habit; sow a habit and you reap a character; sow a character and you reap a destiny."

Charity Versus Self-Righteousness and Self-Glory

When it comes to making personal judgments about ourselves, our circumstances, or others, it is essential that we take a still moment to accurately assess all the facts, offer up a silent prayer for wisdom and inspiration, and consider what is currently in our glass. If we do err in judgment, let it be on the side of mercy. Backwoods lawyer and 16th President of the United States, Abraham Lincoln, once said, "I have always found that mercy bears more fruit than strict judgement."

The Lord's warning to His disciples in His remarkable Sermon on the Mount is clear. In Mathew Chapter 7 we read, "Judge not, that ye be not judged. For with what judgment ye judge, ye shall be judged: and with what measure ye mete, it shall be measured to you again. And why beholdest thou the mote that is in thy brother's eye, but considerest not the beam that is in thine own eye? Or how wilt thou say to thy brother, let me pull out the mote out of thine eye; and behold, a beam is in thine own eye? Thou hypocrite, first cast out the beam out of thine own eye; and then shalt thou see clearly to cast out the mote out of thy brother's eye." (Matthew 7 1:5)

The reality is that man's judgments are subject to human frailties, biases, and false interpretations. If hindsight is 20/20, foresight, reliability, and fallibility are at best 50/50.

Judges play an essential judicious role in our society. They control the tempo within the courtroom, weigh the evidence for both sides, and make judgments that, in many instances, have life-altering effects. In a one-question survey conducted by The National Judicial College and directed to 446 trial judges, 160 or 39% answered the question, "About how often do you disagree with the jury's verdict?" These were their responses:

Less than 25 percent of the time – 82%

26 to 50 percent of the time – 62%

51 to 75 percent of the time – 18%

More than 75 percent of the time – 0%

Average percentage (82%, 62%, 18%) / 3 = 54%

Correct me if I am wrong, but if one trial judge trained in ferreting out the truth of a matter and 12 jurors cannot get it right half of the time, what are the odds that we can?

Although mercy cannot rob justice, it is encouraging to know that when our sojourn in this life has ended, we will stand before our eternal judge and advocate with the Father, to be weighed, measured, and rewarded. Our judge will be an individual who has descended below all things, above all things, and through all things. A person that is infinite in knowledge, infinite in wisdom, and who has perfect judgment.

One of the most difficult challenges we face as parents is when to apply the brakes of justice and the gas pedal of mercy. Justice, like a car break, is used to slow or stop the vehicle to avoid harm to the passenger or passengers within. Mercy, on the other hand, is like the vehicle's gas pedal (or electric pedal if you drive a Prius or Tesla) and is used to provide forward motion. Both are required to drive the vehicle and arrive safely at the intended destination.

Justice and mercy are equal co-partners and essential qualities that will make parenting easier and children's emotional states feel safer and more secure. Each of these traits is equally important. Although justice may appear cold, insensitive, and tough, mercy can appear oversensitive, soft, and even counter-productive in correcting harmful behavior. Yet both are seated in love, and a proper balance of these principles helps create peace and harmony for emotionally stable homes.

The Prophet Isaiah's words best explain the development and value of these attributes by describing the Savior's attributes. That description is in the book of Isaiah of the Old Testament. Beginning in chapter 53, verse 2, we read, "For he shall grow up before him as a tender plant, and as a root out of a dry ground: he hath no form nor comeliness; and when we shall see him, there is no beauty that we should desire him."

Without much effort, we can envision the image of a tender plant next to a dry root coming forth out of the dry ground. Such was the character of Jesus Chris, who, with physical strength and a sense of justice, threw the moneychangers from the temple. Yet, with great tenderness, He also extended mercy to the sinner, forgiveness to the sinner, and tenderness to the children.

CHAPTER 13

A Purpose-Full Life

For the vast majority of us, our lives will be filled with steep climbs, rapid descents, adrenalin rushes, fear, exhilaration, worry, doubt, moments of gratitude, and times of regret. We may find we are up-side-down, inside-out, or even questioning why we decided to board this wild ride. Life can certainly be a roller-coaster experience!

One thing is certain. No matter how hard we are emotionally impacted, we can have some peace of mind knowing that the journey we are on will, at some point, take us back to the point from which we began. And there we can express a sigh of relief and say to ourselves and others, "I Did It!"

My Personal Rollercoaster

For whatever reason, unbeknownst to me at that time, but now much clearer when I am looking through the rearview mirror, the first three years of my mortal life was a roller coaster with a steep ascent, a wicked fast descent, countless twists and turns, and unfortunately a few upside-down experiences.

In essence, my mother wanted a home, a family, and security, while my father wanted freedom, independence, and minimal parental responsibilities. Their marriage ended in divorce when I was three years old. My homemaker mother then entered the workplace full time to feed us and keep a roof overhead. My brother Paul and I became transferees for the next ten years, while my mother desperately looked for a new husband to support us.

Our small family of three would move seven times over the next ten years. The final move took us from my most favorite home in Altadena, California, to my least favorite city in Whittier, California. Here is where our new stepfather Gary, a Los Angeles police officer, chose to live in order to be closer to his aging parents, who lived in nearby Downey.

There were two bright spots in all the moves we made before I reached my teenage years. That was because two of my favorite places on earth at the time were within walking distance of my home. One was a frontiersman looking place called Knott's Berry Farm and the other a whimsical and magical place known as Disneyland. At the first amusement park, my favorite thing to do was pan for gold. The second place had a haunted mansion that was pretty cool. In the end, I gravitated more toward Disneyland due to a unique ride that made me feel like I was older than I was. It was called Autopia and was in a place called Tomorrow Land.

Although the line was usuriously long, the ride was relatively short, depending on how fast you chose to drive. The scenery was almost negligible, but the ride's primary draw was in breaking the rules, especially rule #4, and crossing the finish line before your buddy did. The rules all revolved around safety. #1) If your car breaks down, remain in your vehicle and we will come and help you. #2)

Remain seated at all times. #3) Keep your hands inside the vehicle at all times. #4) Do not crash into the car in front of you.

The first time I drove at the Autopia, I was convinced that the track was filled with delinquents, since all the drivers were crashing into the back of the cars in front of them. I soon joined the crowd and took every chance I got to administer whiplash to every driver in front of me that I deemed was driving too slowly. If it were not for those heavy-duty shock-absorbing bumpers, the ride surely would have been closed for health, safety, and legal reasons.

Like the Autopia bumper guards, our spiritual health, safety, and eternal progression are founded on six fundamental learning principles. These blessings are the primary reasons we chose the vicissitudes of mortality, nobility, and an eternal reward, rather than a life of ease, stagnation, apathy, and a lessor kingdom in the unknown universe. Each principle is essential for our spiritual learning and eternal progression. Following these principles help us to fill the measure of our creation and have joy in the journey. A simple acronym makes it easy to remember these protective guards that will lead us toward eternal life. The acronym is B.U.M.P.E.R.

> B represents Body, or more specifically, the physical bodies that house our spirits. The scriptures refer to these spiritual encases as tabernacles or vessels that house our spirits and facilitate spiritual learning. Without a tangible body, we could not learn about opposing forces such as pain and suffering, sickness and health, or sorrow and joy. These bodies we have been given are essential for each of us to cultivate personal gifts and strengths, increase

knowledge, grow and progress spiritually, and raise our consciousness of who we are and what we can become. The choices we make directly influence and impact our ability to reach our divine potential and freedom of choice agency. Without physical bodies, our spirits are limited in their ability to progress eternally.

U represents Uncover, as in the ability to Uncover something hidden or unseen. Who we were in the pre-existence and why we chose to come here to live in mortality are two fundamental principles that caused us to shout for joy in our premortal existence at the thought of coming here to learn and progress eternally. As we eliminate perceived boundaries and pass beyond our fears and supposed shortcomings, our identities begin to manifest and we see clearly who we are and what we can achieve.

M represents Multiply. In Genesis 1:28 (KJV Old Testament), we read, "And God blessed them, and God said unto them, Be fruitful and multiply, and replenish the earth, and subdue it: and have dominion over the fish of the sea, and over the fowl of the air, and over every living thing that moveth upon the earth."

One of the greatest sources of joy and sorrow will come through our posterity. Healthy parenting is the most difficult responsibility we will ever experience in this life. And yet, it brings with it the greatest joy and satisfaction. It can be especially challenging for those who lacked a conducive home environment in their own upbringing. Successful parenting can become a restorative, rejuvenating, and self-fulfilling experience. Or it can be a humbling, retrospective, learning lesson with the impact and power to cause a loving and eternal Father in Heaven to weep.

P represents Prove. We came here to prove ourselves. Mortality is the greatest proving ground we will ever experience. We are meant to be tested and to learn obedience, sacrifice, and how to consecrate our gifts and talents for the benefits of God's children. We are here to learn to endure all things. We chose in the premortal world to follow Christ and to do the will of our Heavenly Father.

E represents Eternal Progression. Our overwhelming desire in the pre-existence was to progress spiritually and become more like our Father in Heaven. There are only two directions we can go as it pertains to eternal progression. Either we are moving forward, or we are moving backward.

R represents Repentance. The end goal in our coming here is change. By choosing to enter mortality, we agreed to perfect ourselves to one day be worthy to return to the presence of our Father in Heaven, clothed in immortality and eternal life, having filled the measure of our creation and overcome the test of mortality. Our deeds and actions would have little merit if it were not for the atoning sacrifice of the son of God. It is His infinite love for you and me that affords us the invaluable gift of repentance and forgiveness. With these two, His gift, and the mercy wrought by the Savior's Atonement, we are able to change our habits, our course, and our very nature.

BUMPER guards are spiritual principles of protection, purpose, and promise.

CHAPTER 14

The Unsung Heroes

This chapter is dedicated to the many men and women who stayed the course, sacrificing their time, talents, and quite often their financial resources to help another. These are they whom the Savior spoke of in His remarkable Sermon on the Mount, as recorded in Matthew 5.

It is fitting that the Master's foundational lesson to His recently called and ordained disciples would be added to holy writ and affectionately become known as the "B Attitudes." This was a powerful teaching moment that He begins by laying a mental and spiritual foundation of the qualities that lead to perfection. They are the key to becoming a new creature in Christ.

The message is an invitation for all God's children to "Come and See," for ourselves. Put the God of Heaven to the test, do His will and learn the truth of His word. The chapter ends with a call of authenticity and this charge, "Be ye therefore perfect, even as your Father which is in Heaven is perfect."

This chapter honors the memory of those individuals who, regardless of the circumstances, the consequences, or the pains they would endure, stepped up and did what was right because they knew it was right.

These are the unsung heroes, the ones who risked their lives and saved people without the world knowing. You will find these unique NGOs in homes, shelters, and hospitals around the world. These noble and great ones step up their game and rise to an unprecedented level of performance. They do so with full purpose of heart and put forth near extraordinary effort and passionate vigor to help those in need.

You will find them in every discipline and venue we have previously discussed. In nearly every instance, these unsung heroes shunned what they deem is unearned recognition. These Christian Soldiers marched onward until victory was won. When their battles ended, they refrained from personal glory and reveling in their own accomplishments. Rather than seek praise, personal gain, or self-glory, they choose to mourn the loss of their fallen comrades.

The suffering and hardships these humble giants endured, the collateral damage they witnessed, and the miracles they observed laid a path for greater dependency and a stronger relationship with their maker. Their faith is unwavering, their compassion for those that face similar adversity is genuine and heartfelt, and their dependency on a power greater than themselves is true.

Their vessels are overflowing with an over-abundance of noble traits by which they are known, including courage, humility, faith, and gratitude, to name just a few.

Formed by the flame of adversity and purged by the furnace of affliction, these gifted NGOs have forged within themselves a greater sense of purpose, a kinship with longsuffering, and an unending supply of charity for those in need.

As you reflect upon those that have influenced your life in a positive and enriching way, you may want to create your own list of unsung heroes. Some may have passed on, others may have relocated, and some you may even have forgotten. If you still have contact, give them a call, send them a note, or if nothing else, shoot them an email or text message. Thank them for the difference they made in your life. There are at least a dozen major holidays in which we recognize veterans that have served within the United States. There are another 50 lesser-known holidays for service recognition.

Here is the list I compiled:

James Bradley, a Corpsman in WWII. It is estimated that 70,000 U.S soldiers fought in the Battle of Iwo Jima. Survivors described the experience as fighting an unseen enemy.

The beaches had been described as "excellent," and the thrust inland was expected to be "easy." In reality, after crossing the beach, the Marines were faced with 15-foot-high slopes of soft black volcanic ash. This ash allowed for neither a secure footing nor the construction of foxholes to protect them from hostile fire. However, the ash did help to absorb some of the fragments from Japanese artillery.

The Nano Bunker (Southern Area Islands Naval Air HQ), located east of Airfield Number 2, had enough food, water, and ammunition for the Japanese to hold out for three months. The bunker was 90 feet deep, with tunnels running in various directions. Approximately 500 55-gallon drums filled with water, kerosene, and fuel oil for generators were located inside the complex. Gasoline-powered generators allowed for radios and lighting to be operated underground.

By February 19, 1945, the day the Americans invaded, 18 kilometers (11 miles) of a planned 27 kilometers (17 miles) of tunnel network had been dug. Adjacent to the Nano Bunker were numerous command centers and barracks 75 feet beneath the ground. Tunnels allowed troop movement between these sites and various defense positions to go undetected. Hundreds of hidden artillery and mortar positions, along with land mines, were placed all across the island. Among the Japanese weapons were 320mm spigot mortars and a variety of explosive rockets.

Nonetheless, the Japanese supply was inadequate. Their troops were supplied 60% of the standard issue of ammunition sufficient for one engagement by one division, plus food and forage for four months. Numerous Japanese snipers and camouflaged machine gun positions were also set up. The Japanese commander engineered the defenses so that every part of Iwo Jima was subject to Japanese defensive fire. He also received a handful of kamikaze pilots to use against the enemy fleet. Kamikaze attacks killed 318 American sailors during the battle.

Marines were trained to move rapidly forward; here, they could only plod. The weight and amount of equipment carried were a huge hindrance, and various items were rapidly discarded. First to go were the gas masks.

Here is one account from the ordeal of 2nd Lt. Benjamin Roselle, part of a ground team directing naval gunfire. "Within a minute, a mortar shell exploded among the group...his left foot and ankle hung from his leg, held on by a ribbon of flesh. Within minutes, a second round landed near him and fragments tore into his other leg. For nearly an hour, he wondered where the next shell would land."

He was soon to find out as a shell burst almost on top of him, wounding him for the third time in the shoulder. Almost at once, another explosion bounced him several feet into the air and hot shards ripped into both thighs. As he lifted his arm to look at his watch, a mortar shell exploded only feet away and blasted the watch from his wrist and tore a large and jagged hole in his forearm. "I was beginning to know what it must be like to be crucified," he later said. Time-Life correspondent Robert Sherrod described it simply as "a nightmare in hell."

The Medal of Honor is the highest military decoration awarded by the United States government. It is bestowed on a member of the United States armed forces who distinguishes himself by "...conspicuous gallantry and intrepidity at the risk of his life above and beyond the call of duty while engaged in an action against an enemy of the United States." Because of its nature, the medal is commonly awarded posthumously. Since its creation during the American Civil War, it has been presented only 3,525 times and awarded to only 3,506 individuals.

The Medal of Honor was awarded to 22 U.S. Marines and five sailors (14 posthumously) after the battle of Iwo Jima. These 22 Medals of Honor accounted for 28% of the 82 awarded to Marines in World War II.

James Bradley received the Navy Cross for his bravery in the battle, but his children were unaware until his death. Bradley was not boastful about his war experience. As a corpsman, he undoubtedly saw the true horrors of bodily injuries. He held life sacred, and while all those around him focused on taking life, his sole purpose was to save them. Each of the three divisions engaged in the struggle for Iwo Jima included roughly 100 Navy surgeons and nearly 1,000 corpsmen in its ranks. That means out of the estimated 70,000 U.S soldiers who fought on Iwo Jima, there were just 3000 corpsmen to rescue, revive, retrieve, and return these soldiers to a surgeon's care. The nature of their work required continuous risk-taking. They retrieved wounded Marines, performed initial life-saving measures, and evacuated severe casualties back to the beach — always under fire.

Navy medical crews paid an exorbitant price in the savage fighting at Iwo Jima. Twenty-three doctors and 827 corpsmen were killed or wounded: a casualty rate twice as high as bloody Saipan. Bradley was a casualty of heavy fighting in the northern part of the island 17 days after the historic flag raising.

James Harrison was born and raised in Australia. When he learned he had an unusual plasma composition in his blood that could treat Rhesus disease, he tried to donate blood for the rest of his life. He made over 1000 blood donations, which are estimated to have saved over two million lives.

Harrison decided to donate blood after undergoing a surgery at the age of 14, which required 13 liters of blood. Finding out that he had rare antibodies, which fought and prevented Rhesus disease, he began donating as much blood as possible. He donated blood for 57 years and saved 2.4 million babies. On average, one in ten pregnant women used his blood to prevent the disease.

Vasili Arkhipov was a senior officer on a Soviet submarine. He was second in command of four Soviet submarines when he defied and vetoed his captain's orders to fire a nuclear torpedo at U.S. warships in Cuba without sufficient information.

Due to the depth of the submarine, Moscow was unable to contact the crew for days. Hence the crew was without any update on the brewing Cuba missile crisis situation.

Arkhipov decided they needed to contact headquarters and surfaced the submarine.

The U.S. had administered a naval blockade around Cuba and informed the Soviets in Moscow of some new drills. When Vasili refused his captain's orders, he saved the entire world from entering WWIII. Many in Russia viewed him as a coward and traitor, but his wife and others saw him as a hero. He averted another major war and saved millions of lives.

Nils Bohlin, a Swedish inventor, saved millions of lives with his invention of the modern, three-point safety seat belt while working at Volvo. The patent was given away for free in order to reduce costs. Bohlin's invention saves about 11,000 lives in the U.S. alone each year.

Bohlin introduced the invention in 1959 to his company, which received the first patent. He conducted a study on the safety of the device using 28,000 accidents. The results proved occupants wearing the seat belt did not suffer fatalities nearly as often as those without this safety restraint.

His device became required in all vehicles in the United States. According to one study, the three-point seat belt is estimated to have reduced fatalities in accidents by almost 50%. Bohlin's invention has been used for vehicles, airplanes, and buses.

Geochemist Clair Patterson used lead isotopic data to determine the Earth's age. He also spent decades fighting the industrial use of lead. His efforts helped reduce lead levels in the blood of American workers by approximately 80% by the late 1990s.

During Patterson's studies on the Earth's age, he found numerous samples contaminated with high amounts of lead. With his interest peaked, Patterson obtained samples from Greenland and Antarctica for further studies. He noticed significant increases in lead levels across the world since its use in fuel.

In 1965, Patterson forced the issue into the public domain and fought the gasoline industries to reduce their high lead content.

Patterson's forward thinking led to his exclusion from research councils and organizations. They knew his research could prove harmful to business finances. Despite barriers, Patterson persuaded the U.S. to mandate unleaded gasoline for all new cars from 1975. This reduced lead contamination significantly.

Eugene Lazowski, a Polish doctor, saved 8,000 Jews during the Holocaust by injecting dead typhus cells into them. This enabled them to test positive for typhus despite being healthy. Germans were afraid of the highly contagious typhoid disease and refused to deport them to concentration camps.

After serving in the Polish Army, Lebowski lived in Rozwadow, where he met his friend Dr. Stanislaw Matulewicz, a doctor who had created a way to inject dead typhus cells into people without side effects and still test positive for the disease. Eugene took this discovery and injected Jews in the Rozwadow area.

Germans were terrified of this disease and quarantined the entire town. Stanislaw and Lazowski continued inoculating other villages in the areas of Rozwadow and Zbydniow. Lazowski saved at least 8,000 Polish Jews from concentration camps by frightening Germans with the deadly typhus fever disease.

Neerja Bhanot was a 22-year-old air hostess who helped hide 41 American passports aboard a hijacked plane. She then helped passengers escape and died shielding three children from gunfire. Bhanot was posthumously awarded bravery medals in India, Pakistan, and the United States.

Bhanot was a young hostess for Pan American Flight 73, flying from India to the United States. She noticed hijackers aboard the plane and immediately alerted the cockpit crew. They escaped through a hatch while the terrorists remained aboard.

The four terrorists targeted Americans aboard the plane and intended to fly to Cyprus to free their Palestinian brothers. Neerja secretly gathered the American passports and hid them so the terrorists would not be able to tell the people apart. The terrorist's first victim was an American man. They shot him in the head and tossed him out of the plane. Small bombs started going off and the terrorists shot at the other passengers. Bhanot helped people escape through an exit hatch. Three children were about to exit the hatch when the terrorists noticed her. She shielded the children and was shot dead while saving their lives.

One of the children later went on and became a pilot because he admired her so much. She became the first and youngest woman to receive the Ashoka Chakra Award in India for her bravery.

The Chernobyl "Suicide Squad" were three plant workers who volunteered to go beneath the reactors to release the valves days after the Chernobyl disaster. They waded through the water underneath a leaking reactor to release the safety valves and prevent a chain reaction of nuclear explosions. The molten reactor core was coming ever closer to the water source. The connection of the two would cause a chain reaction of reactor explosions, destroying the entire power station.

Suited up in minimal protection from radiation, the men waded through knee-high water and intense heat to open the valves. They saved 50% of Europe from being wiped out and from being rendered uninhabitable for 500,000 years.

Despite immense pressure from pharmaceutical companies, Dr. Frances Kelsey refused to approve thalidomide for morning sickness in the United States. Her disapproval saved a generation and thousands of children from death and deformities.

Dr. Kelsey, one of seven physicians reviewing drugs for the FDA, denied the approval of thalidomide. The drug caused unknown side effects, specifically to the nervous system. Kelsey required further studies into the side effects of the drug before any further thought of approval.

Pharmaceutical companies pressured Kelsey. They stated pregnant women needed the drug for the treatment of morning sickness. Other nations, such as Canada and some European countries, approved the drug. Pharmaceutical companies in the U.S. thought it would be an instant success. They finally accepted her decision when cases of defective children arose in Europe. Children were born with webbed fingers and feet, or missing arms and legs.

She was the second woman to receive the President's Award for Distinguished Federal Civilian Service.

Aki Ra, a former child soldier in Cambodia, risked his life to destroy and remove landmines with no more than a knife, hoe, and stick. He saved thousands of lives and helped people regain valuable land. Aki also adopted children injured by landmines and those suffering from polio or HIV.

Ra, an orphaned child, enlisted in the army at a young age. After serving in the military, Ra dedicated his life to clearing thousands of landmines in the area around his home in Cambodia. Small villages, overlooked by the UN, benefited from his services. The disarmed landmines uncovered filled Ra's house, which he turned into a museum and charged $1 for admission to help fund his project and help adopt the landmine's young victims. While traveling to disarm landmines, Ra adopted and saved 29 young landmine victims, which stayed in his small Cambodia Landmine Museum Relief Center.

Ra's efforts were temporarily halted when he was jailed for disarming landmines without a certification. This did not stop the young man and inspired him to travel to London, where he gained his certification. Ra was then able to continue disarming landmines in Cambodia legally. In the first year of his certification, Ra helped put over 2,400 people back on their land.

Henrietta Lacks, born to a poor family in Virginia, suffered from cervical cancer and sought medical attention at a Maryland hospital. Without Henrietta's knowledge, the medical staff took samples of her cancerous cells and used them for medical research.

Her cells became the first "immortal cells" to be kept alive for medical use, including creating the polio vaccine to cloning. Known as "HeLa," her cells reproduced rapidly and lasted a long time. Medical researchers used these cells to make new discoveries and advances in cancer, cloning, and gene mapping. Her cells helped create the polio vaccine, which saved thousands of lives.

Scientists around the world sought her cells, which became the first mass-produced cells sold globally. As the demand for her cells grew, researchers took more samples from her body while it lay in the autopsy facility after her death in 1951. Without knowing it, Lacks helped medical research and saved thousands of lives with her contribution to the polio vaccine.

CHAPTER 15

A Heavenly Reunion

The two great bookends of mortality are birth and death. These two transitional events are brief, yet defining, moments that herald and echo divinity throughout eternity.

These two celebratory and reflective moments can evoke powerful and purposeful emotions within us, such as hope, faith, forgiveness, happiness, gratitude, jubilation, peace, protection, and relief. And yet, they also have an influence in evoking difficult and disparaging emotions, such as fear, guilt, remorse, disbelief, denial, depression, doubt, worry, and pain. Welcome to mortality, the preparatory meridian for immortality and eternal life and proving ground for life hereafter.

As parents, we hope our children will be born with good health and under favorable circumstances. In our hearts, and in our minds, we pray they will live long, happy, and prosperous lives. We wonder what challenges they will face or what hurdles they will have to overcome. We wish them fulfillment in the present and endless possibilities for the future.

Under the best of circumstances, the story rarely turns out the way we would have written it. The scriptures are replete and transparent about several fundamental and eternal principles that shed light on where we began, why we are here, and where we ought to be headed.

Prior to your mortal birth, you lived in spirit form in a pre-existent world with your Heavenly Father who created you. Because you are the workmanship of His eternal hands, in the day you were fashioned, even before this earth was formed, He knows and loves you intimately, completely, and unconditionally. Every person on this earth represents a spiritual son or daughter of God, created in His image and likeness and possessing His divine potential.

This eternal truth means that any person you see, hear, or interact with — regardless of race, color, persuasion, nature, circumstance, societal status, or net worth — is literally your eternal brother or sister. If this kinship principle is true, what bearing does it have on how we should treat others, and what accountability or penalty does a parent evoke when a sibling rivalry occurs in a home?

To put things into sharper perspective, in the premortal world, Jesus Christ proposed a plan to His Father for the advancement of His spiritual offspring. That plan included three primary objectives: agency, salvation, and eternal progression. He unselfishly proposed, "Let the glory be thine." Lucifer also presented a plan that was the antithesis of the Savior's plan. At its core were compulsion and spiritual regression. He then selfishly proposed, "Give me the glory." Which plan would you have chosen?

Those of us having a physical body that houses our spirit chose to follow Jesus Christ. When Satan rebelled, he and his minions were cast out of heaven to roam the earth. They are among us today, and he and his followers are relentlessly seeking to thwart the plan of the Savior and make all men and women as miserable as they are.

Our mortal birth represents a passage of entry into this proving ground and probationary period we call earth life. We knew the syllabus before we came here. It would not be easy; we would face challenges and opposition. But scripture supports that we shouted for joy at the opportunity and blessings mortality would provide for our future development.

Lucifer began his disobedience to his Heavenly Father in the pre-existence, and continued his assault on our first parents, tempting Adam first, then Eve to partake of the forbidden fruit. In her wisdom and intuition, Eve partook and then convinced Adam to partake, so they could remain a couple and they with their future posterity could learn through earthly experiences to choose right from wrong, good versus evil, and sorrow verses joy. Free agency and opposition in all things are two fundamental principles that accelerate, decelerate, or prohibit our eternal progression.

The nearsighted, ignorance, and error in judgment by Lucifer could not have been more beneficial to the faithful sons and daughters of God. Our desire to please our Father in Heaven, accept the Savior's plan of salvation, and subject ourselves to the vicissitudes of mortality are evidence of our valiancy in the preexistence.

It took the intellect, intuition, and pure brilliance of Eve, an NGO who saw the wisdom of partaking of the forbidden fruit. It was a deliberate act in direct opposition to a commandment given by the Father that would subject all mankind to health and sickness, pleasure and pain, joy and sadness, and necessitate a redeemer to atone for our sins. It also allows us to repent and change our course and return to the presence of our Eternal Father. It was an act that would demand a ransom be made.

The Atonement wrought by Jesus Christ, the indescribable and unfathomable pain and suffering He endured in Gethsemane for you and me, and the residual impact and opportunity it provides us to acknowledge our weaknesses and shortcomings, to feel sorrow for our actions, make restitution for our mistakes, and to ask forgiveness from those whom we offend is a debt we can never repay.

The atonement of Jesus Christ broke the bands of death as He became the first fruits of those that slept, providing us a way through and beyond every adversity we may experience in this life, a means to acquire the knowledge that all things have opposites. The experiences we have in mortality and the knowledge we acquire here affords the acquisition of wisdom.

The Atonement gave us the key to eternity and a way for us to return to our Father in Heaven. It represents prophesy fulfilled, infinite compassion, and endless mercy. The Atonement of Jesus Christ was the noblest and greatest act ever rendered by a Son of God on behalf of His children.

No father will ever be more pleased in his son that the Father was for His beloved son Jesus Christ. No son will ever be more grateful, loyal, and obedient in following the will of his father than Jesus was toward His Father in Heaven. They were inseparable, of one mind and one heart.

The life, mission, and the atonement of Jesus Christ place Him at the top of the list as the most Noble and Greatest individual in the heavens, on earth, and throughout all eternity.

Well did the prophet Isaiah prophesy, "For unto us a child is born, unto us a son is given and the government shall be upon his shoulder: and his name shall be called Wonderful, Counsellor, The mighty God, The everlasting Father, The Prince of Peace." (Isaiah 9:6)

Your future is bright, your origin divine, and the gifts and talents within you were given to you by a loving Father with the intent that they are used to bless the lives of His children. As you find and fulfill the measure of your creation, acknowledging your unique and distinguishing features, your joy will increase, the Light of Christ or conscience within you will grow, and your countenance will shine as in the heavens. You will come to know your true value, your true potential, and your love for all God's children.

The Father and the Son have a perfect love for each one of us. They cheer for us when we have success. They weep for us when we regress and struggle. I believe that when our life here in mortality is completed, we will pass beyond the veil of mortality and into the presence of passed loved ones that have longingly awaited our return. The moment will be jubilant, the tenor will be one of gratitude, and the forgiveness endless. There will be no time or room for accusations, no time or room for blame, no callous self-righteous judgment, no time for excuses, and no time to repent and make restitution.

There will only be time to embrace our loved ones with tears of gratitude and words of thanksgiving for their sacrifices made on our behalf.

As we enter the presence of our Savior Jesus Christ, He will greet us with outstretched arms, and we will fall at His feet and worship Him for the Nobility and Greatness of His life and the infinite Atonement he suffered for us. At that moment, we will be at a loss for words, nor would they be necessary, or of any import. We will be choked by emotion; our hearts will feel like breaking for being in the presence of The Noble and Great One.

Our tears will wash His feet in adoration and our gratitude overflowing. When He speaks to us His words will be merciful yet just, soft yet powerful, forgiving yet resolute. His judgment will be just and His mercy will be bountiful.

I add my personal witness of His Nobility and Greatness. In the Garden of Gethsemane, seated between the empty tomb on my left and the hill of Golgotha on my right, I sat reflecting on the holy sites we had visited, the scriptures we had read and the hymns we had sung during the span of a two-day excursion in Israel.

Our tour guide invited us to sing one last hymn before our departure home to the United States. You may be familiar with the hymn. It was written by Carl Boberg and is called *How Great Thou Art*.

As we began singing, I noticed my mind became flooded by emotion, my throat became restricted and, as we reached the middle of the third stanza I could no longer sing or speak. Tears welled up in my eyes as the spirit bore witness to me of the nobility and greatness of the Savior of all mankind. His teachings, His love, His ministry, His atonement, His death, His glorious resurrection, and His ascension back into the presence of the Father were indelibly ingrained in my mind and in my heart. It was a moment I will always treasure, revere, and keep sacred.

As we left the garden, I took one last look at the empty tomb and received one final impression that angles still frequent this hallowed place.

Dialogue

May you remember the acronyms and credos you have learned in this book. May they be a protection to you, may they guide your thoughts and choices and may they help keep you on a path of purposeful living on your journey through mortality.

May the individuals, principles, and examples shared in these pages inspire you to find your own true identity and stay the course of the nobility and greatness within you. May you remain on the straight and narrow path that will lead you safely back to the presence of your Eternal Father in Heaven.

There is nobility and greatness within you. You have the ability and the grace of God to repent of your sins, change your stance, and fill the measure of your creation. No matter what circumstances you may be facing, what trials you are enduring, or what sins you have committed, the power to change course is within you and the reason you are here is change itself.

There is no time or need for pity parties, judging others and labeling those that see things differently than you do. There is no time or need for envying others. There is only time to be thankful for what you have and giving what you can give freely.

Your time is precious! If you are sad, lonely, or feeling short-changed by life, repent, make a change, go in a different direction, and stop comparing yourself to others.

Above all, remember, "It's not about proportions, it's what's in the glass that matters most." You are a child of God. Divinity is in your very nature. You are here at this moment by divine decree and purpose.

Now get out of your comfort zone and become the person you were meant to be. Fill the measure of your creation and have more joy than you could ever have imagined.

It is up to you! Your Heavenly Father believes in you and longs for your triumphant return into His outstretched loving arms.

Find out what is truly in your glass and find your true destiny!

Acknowledgments

The Men in my life:

Demar Barron, one of the most charitable men I have ever known. A true disciple of Jesus Christ who emulates His teaching and lives life to the fullest.

John Chipman, who believed in me, mentored me, and took a chance on me when I needed encouragement, wisdom, and direction.

John Evans, who lives his life with nobility, greatness, and meekness. A spiritual giant among God's children and a person I will physically and spiritually always look up to.

Bob Meyers, who managed Multiple Sclerosis (MS) over the 18 years we knew each other, and who always knew what, when, and how to say the right thing at the perfect moment.

Jack Renouf, whose compassion and concern for my welfare was always consistent, sincere, and heartfelt.

Keith Sullivan, the hardest working man I have ever known. He lived life to the fullest, rode a Husqvarna Motorcycle, and drove a Shelby Mustang when we first met. Need I say more?

Joshua Colo, my only son, my sensei, my counselor, and a peacemaker in our home.

The Women in my life:

Joan B. Glad, my counselor who helped me find my happy thoughts following my third broken engagement at age 35.

Mary Colo, who, in a weakened moment, agreed to marry me and support me despite all my weaknesses and shortcomings.

Rachel Colo, my firstborn child. An INTJ (Myers Briggs) and "D" personality (DISC Personality Profile) type, just like her Dad! Who made me a father!

Lauren Colo, our third child, the icing on the cake, who has taught me to refrain from judgment, treat all mankind with dignity and respect, and live life to the fullest.

About the Author

Mark Colo has a long history of volunteerism. He is one of the four Founders of Find Neuro Help, formerly known as FINDcures. This newly branded foundation is a 501 (c) 3 non-profit organization committed to finding help for individuals with chronic neuro-diseases who need goods and services beyond what most healthcare plans will cover.

Our strategic alliances and service providers subsidize the costs associated with these services. The patron can be assured that the cost of these services is well below the market and, in many instances, pro bono. If you were to explain what we do, tell the inquiring party that Find Neuro Help is similar to Aflac. We provide transitional support that remedies the patient's foremost concerns. As a Parkinson's patient, Mark is passionate about the Find Neuro Help mission.

In January 1977, while still a teenager, he volunteered to leave his home in sunny Southern California to serve for two years as a full-time missionary in the significantly colder climate of Scotland and Northern Ireland during that region's intense civil unrest.

Of serving others while as a missionary, Mark says, "The greatest lesson I learned about serving my fellow man is the more I help others, the happier I am, and the greater my sense of identity and purpose can become. I also learned that giving of myself to others has the effect of lifting me above my doubt, worry, and potholes of despair, to a higher plane of thought. Simply put, by losing myself in serving others, I found my true self."

While serving the wonderful people of Scotland and Northern Ireland, Mark began to form what became his top four credos of life. First, "The only constant is change. Embrace it." Second, "If you think things cannot get worse, you're wrong. Endure it." Third, "Control is an illusion. Let go of it." And fourth, "Life isn't always fair. Accept it."

As fate would have it, these four concepts, along with his undying faith in a loving God, have been a source of strength for him as he has dealt with the ongoing challenges of Parkinson's disease.

Mark provides a unique perspective to the Find Neuro Help Leadership Team, as he is intimately aware of the challenges an individual and their family face when dealing with a neurological disease diagnosis.

Professionally, Mark has had an extraordinarily successful career in the relocation industry since January 1980. During his four decades of experience in the relocation industry, he leveraged his passion for learning to become a Certified Relocation Professional (CRP). There are fewer than 200 CRPs in the U.S. He is also a licensed California

Real Estate Broker. In addition, his dedication to client satisfaction resulted in him becoming a 5-time member of the United Van Lines Masters Club. This distinction put him in the top 5% of his peers nationwide.

Over the course of his career, Mark has relocated more than 15,000 families to all points in the United States and overseas. He has also helped relocate 300 businesses and 100 scientists and their medical research laboratories.

In his personal life, Mark enjoys spending time with his family, cycling, overseas travel, reading, and furthering public awareness of Neurological Diseases. He is the author of *Peace with Parkinson's – It is Called a Resting Tremor, not an Earthquake*, available on Amazon. Proceeds from the sale of this book will be distributed to individuals with neuro-diseases.

Made in the USA
Las Vegas, NV
08 August 2022